中华人民共和国

2021年国民经济和社会发展统计公报

STATISTICAL COMMUNIQUÉ OF THE PEOPLE'S REPUBLIC OF CHINA ON THE 2021 NATIONAL ECONOMIC AND SOCIAL DEVELOPMENT

国家统计局
National Bureau of Statistics of China

2022年2月28日
February 28, 2022

中国统计出版社
China Statistics Press

图书在版编目（CIP）数据

中华人民共和国 2021 年国民经济和社会发展统计公报 = Statistical Communiqué of the People' s Republic of China on the 2021 National Economic and Social Development : 汉英对照 / 国家统计局编 . -- 北京 : 中国统计出版社 , 2022.3
ISBN 978-7-5037-9789-7

Ⅰ . ①中… Ⅱ . ①国… Ⅲ . ①国民经济发展－统计资料－公报－中国－ 2021 －汉、英②社会发展－统计资料－公报－中国－ 2021 －汉、英 Ⅳ . ① F124-66

中国版本图书馆 CIP 数据核字 (2022) 第 033182 号

中华人民共和国 2021 年国民经济和社会发展统计公报

作　　者 / 国家统计局
责任编辑 / 郭　栋
装帧设计 / 黄　晨
出版发行 / 中国统计出版社有限公司
通信地址 / 北京市丰台区西三环南路甲 6 号　邮政编码 /100073
发行电话 / 邮购（010）63376909　书店（010）68783171
网　　址 / http://www.zgtjcbs.com/
印　　刷 / 北京画中画印刷有限公司
经　　销 / 新华书店
开　　本 / 880mm×1230mm　1/16
字　　数 / 92 千字
印　　张 / 5
版　　别 / 2022 年 3 月第 1 版
版　　次 / 2022 年 3 月第 1 次印刷
定　　价 / 38.00 元

目录

CONTENTS

中华人民共和国
2021年国民经济和社会发展统计公报[1]

国家统计局
2022年2月28日

2021年是党和国家历史上具有里程碑意义的一年。在以习近平同志为核心的党中央坚强领导下，各地区各部门坚持以习近平新时代中国特色社会主义思想为指导，全面贯彻党的十九大和十九届历次全会精神，弘扬伟大建党精神，按照党中央、国务院决策部署，坚持稳中求进工作总基调，完整、准确、全面贯彻新发展理念，加快构建新发展格局，全面深化改革开放，坚持创新驱动发展，推动高质量发展。我们隆重庆祝中国共产党成立一百周年，实现第一个百年奋斗目标，开启向第二个百年奋斗目标进军新征程，沉着应对百年变局和世纪疫情，构建新发展格局迈出新步伐，高质量发展取得新成效，实现了“十四五”良好开局。我国经济发展和疫情防控保持全球领先地位，国家战略科技力量加快壮大，产业链韧性得到提升，改革开放向纵深推进，民生保障有力有效，生态文明建设持续推进。这些成绩的取得，是以习近平同志为核心的党中央坚强领导的结果，是全党全国各族人民勠力同心、艰苦奋斗的结果。

---

[1] 本公报中数据均为初步统计数。各项统计数据均未包括香港特别行政区、澳门特别行政区和台湾省。部分数据因四舍五入的原因，存在总计与分项合计不等的情况。

一、综合

初步核算，全年国内生产总值[2]1143670亿元，比上年增长8.1%，两年平均增长[3]5.1%。其中，第一产业增加值83086亿元，比上年增长7.1%；第二产业增加值450904亿元，增长8.2%；第三产业增加值609680亿元，增长8.2%。第一产业增加值占国内生产总值比重为7.3%，第二产业增加值比重为39.4%，第三产业增加值比重为53.3%。全年最终消费支出拉动国内生产总值增长5.3个百分点，资本形成总额拉动国内生产总值增长1.1个百分点，货物和服务净出口拉动国内生产总值增长1.7个百分点。全年人均国内生产总值80976元，比上年增长8.0%。国民总收入[4]1133518亿元，比上年增长7.9%。全员劳动生产率[5]为146380元/人，比上年提高8.7%。

图1 2017-2021年国内生产总值及其增长速度

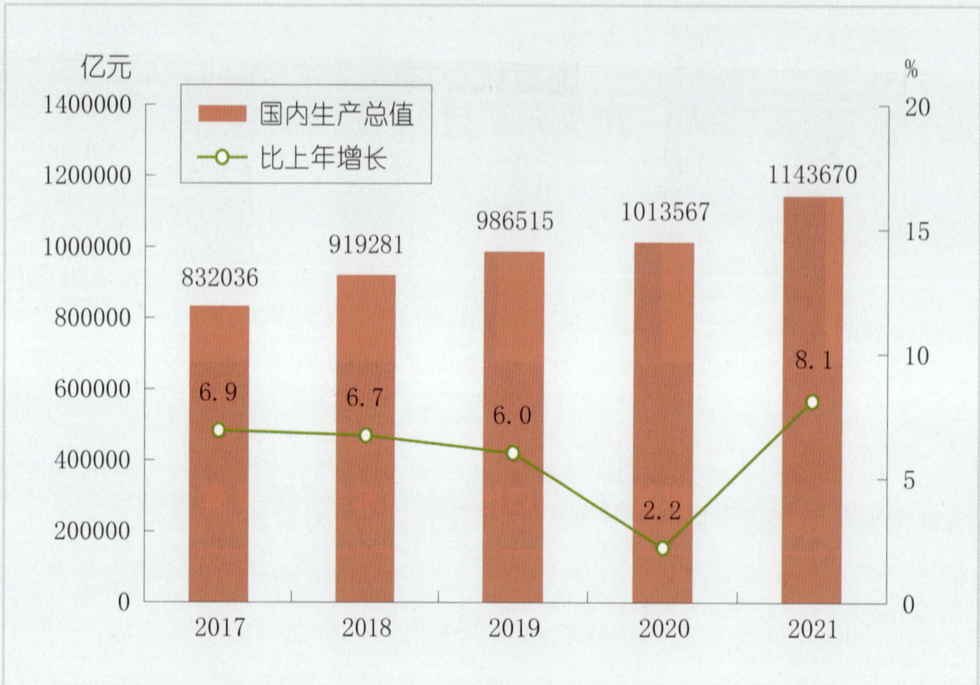

[2] 国内生产总值、三次产业及相关行业增加值、地区生产总值、人均国内生产总值和国民总收入绝对数按现价计算，增长速度按不变价格计算。

[3] 两年平均增速是指以2019年同期数为基数，采用几何平均的方法计算的增速。

[4] 国民总收入，原称国民生产总值，是指一个国家或地区所有常住单位在一定时期内所获得的初次分配收入总额，等于国内生产总值加上来自国外的初次分配收入净额。

[5] 全员劳动生产率为国内生产总值（按2020年价格计算）与全部就业人员的比率，根据第七次全国人口普查结果对历史数据进行了修订。

图 2　2017–2021 年三次产业增加值占国内生产总值比重

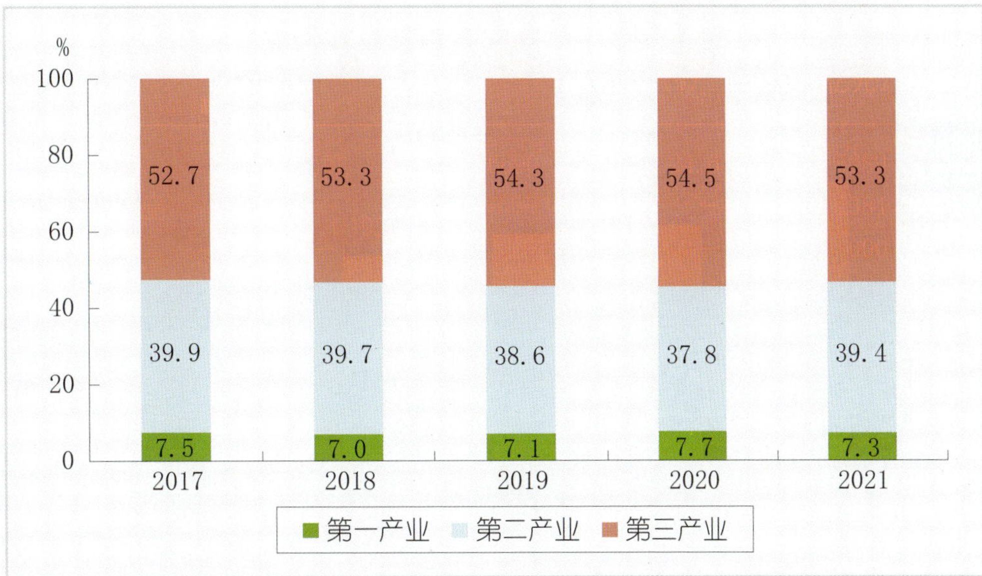

图 3　2017–2021 年全员劳动生产率[6]

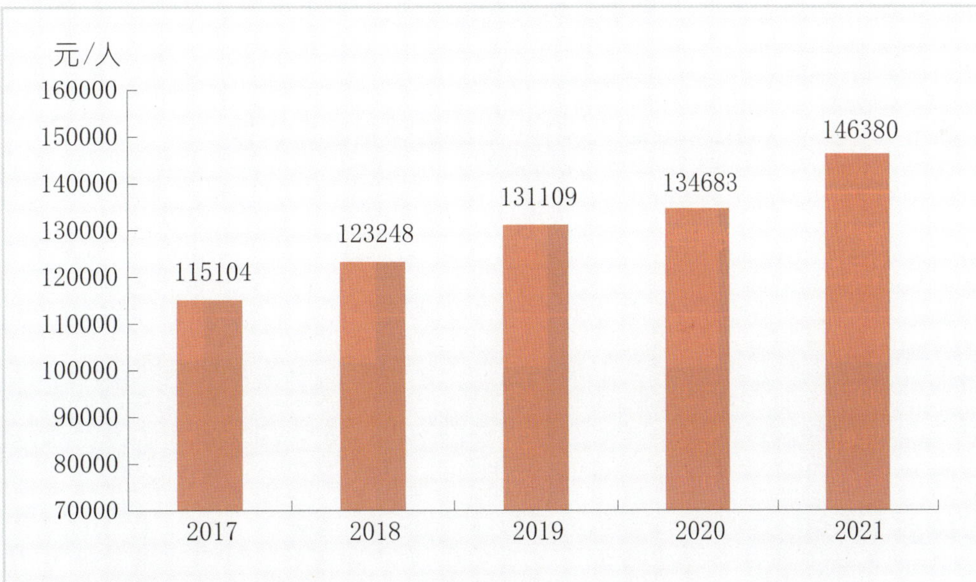

年末全国人口[7]141260万人，比上年末增加48万人，其中城镇常住人口91425万人。全年出生人口1062万人，出生率为7.52‰；死亡人口1014万人，死亡率为7.18‰；自然增长率为0.34‰。全国

[6] 见注释 [5]。

[7] 全国人口是指我国大陆 31 个省、自治区、直辖市和现役军人的人口，不包括居住在 31 个省、自治区、直辖市的港澳台居民和外籍人员。

人户分离的人口[8]5.04亿人，其中流动人口[9]3.85亿人。

表1 2021年年末人口数及其构成

指 标	年末数（万人）	比重（%）
全国人口	141260	100.0
其中：城镇	91425	64.7
乡村	49835	35.3
其中：男性	72311	51.2
女性	68949	48.8
其中：0-15岁（含不满16周岁）[10]	26302	18.6
16-59岁（含不满60周岁）	88222	62.5
60周岁及以上	26736	18.9
其中：65周岁及以上	20056	14.2

年末全国就业人员74652万人，其中城镇就业人员46773万人，占全国就业人员比重为62.7%，比上年末上升1.1个百分点。全年城镇新增就业1269万人，比上年多增83万人。全年全国城镇调查失业率平均值为5.1%。年末全国城镇调查失业率为5.1%，城镇登记失业率为3.96%。全国农民工[11]总量29251万人，比上年增长2.4%。其中，外出农民工17172万人，增长1.3%；本地农民工12079万人，增长4.1%。

图4 2017—2021年城镇新增就业人数

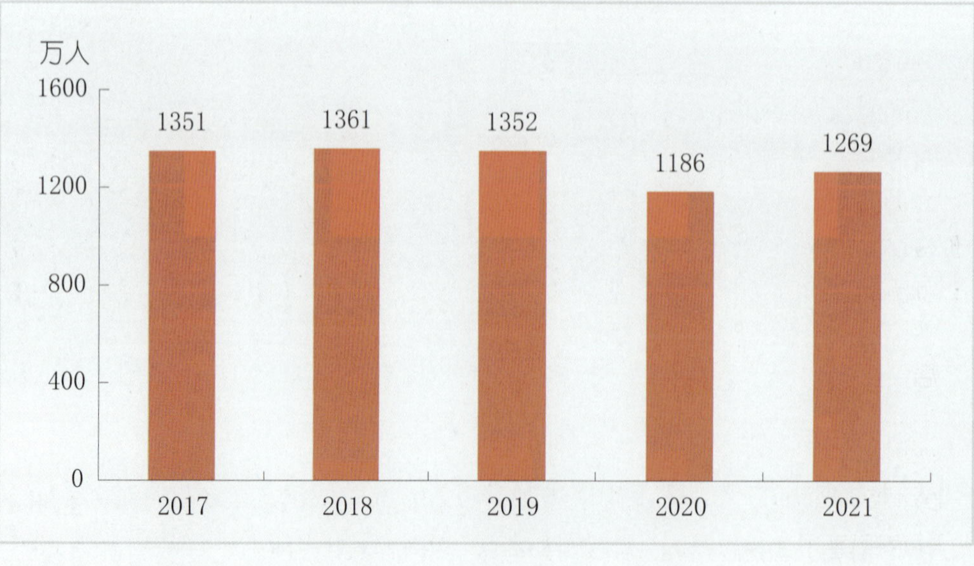

[8]人户分离的人口是指居住地与户口登记地所在的乡镇街道不一致且离开户口登记地半年及以上的人口。

[9]流动人口是指人户分离人口中扣除市辖区内人户分离的人口。市辖区内人户分离的人口是指一个直辖市或地级市所辖区内和区与区之间，居住地和户口登记地不在同一乡镇街道的人口。

[10]2021年年末，0—14岁（含不满15周岁）人口为24678万人，15—59岁（含不满60周岁）人口为89846万人。

[11]年度农民工数量包括年内在本乡镇以外从业6个月及以上的外出农民工和在本乡镇内从事非农产业6个月及以上的本地农民工。

全年居民消费价格比上年上涨0.9%。工业生产者出厂价格上涨8.1%。工业生产者购进价格上涨11.0%。农产品生产者价格[12]下降2.2%。12月份，70个大中城市中，新建商品住宅销售价格同比上涨的城市个数为53个，下降的为17个；二手住宅销售价格同比上涨的城市个数为43个，持平的为1个，下降的为26个。

图5　2021年居民消费价格月度涨跌幅度

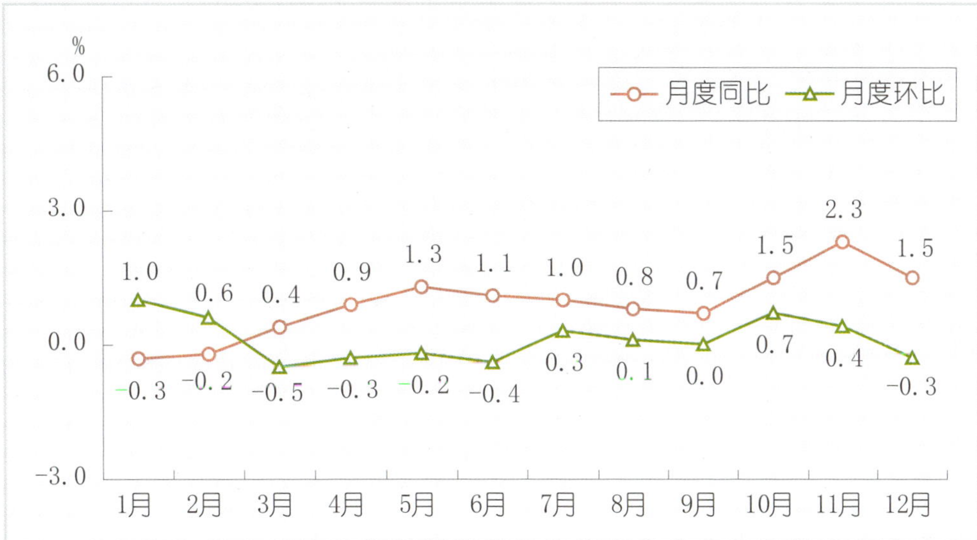

表2　2021年居民消费价格比上年涨跌幅度

单位：%

指　标	全　国	城　市	农　村
居民消费价格	0.9	1.0	0.7
其中：食品烟酒	-0.3	0.0	-1.2
衣　着	0.3	0.3	0.0
居　住[13]	0.8	0.8	1.1
生活用品及服务	0.4	0.4	0.4
交通通信	4.1	4.2	3.9
教育文化娱乐	1.9	2.0	1.7
医疗保健	0.4	0.3	0.7
其他用品及服务	-1.3	-1.4	-1.2

[12] 农产品生产者价格是指农产品生产者直接出售其产品时的价格。
[13] 居住类价格包括租赁房房租、住房保养维修及管理、水电燃料等价格。

年末国家外汇储备32502亿美元，比上年末增加336亿美元。全年人民币平均汇率为1美元兑6.4515元人民币，比上年升值6.9%。

图6 2017-2021年年末国家外汇储备

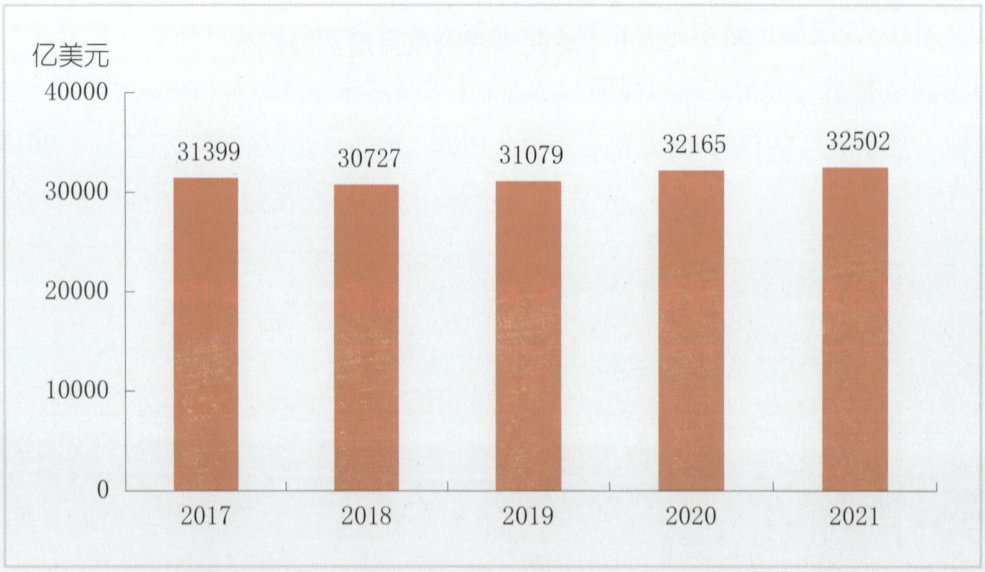

新产业新业态新模式加速成长。全年规模以上工业中，高技术制造业[14]增加值比上年增长18.2%，占规模以上工业增加值的比重为15.1%；装备制造业[15]增加值增长12.9%，占规模以上工业增加值的比重为32.4%。全年规模以上服务业[16]中，战略性新兴服务业[17]企业营业收入比上年增长16.0%。全年高技术产业投资[18]比上年增长17.1%。全年新能源汽车产量367.7万辆，比上年增长152.5%；集成电路产量3594.3亿块，增长37.5%。全年网上零售额[19]130884亿元，按可比口径计算，比上年增长14.1%。全年新登记市场主体2887万户，日均新登记企业2.5万户，年末市场主体总数达1.5亿户。

[14] 高技术制造业包括医药制造业，航空、航天器及设备制造业，电子及通信设备制造业，计算机及办公设备制造业，医疗仪器设备及仪器仪表制造业，信息化学品制造业。

[15] 装备制造业包括金属制品业，通用设备制造业，专用设备制造业，汽车制造业，铁路、船舶、航空航天和其他运输设备制造业，电气机械和器材制造业，计算机、通信和其他电子设备制造业，仪器仪表制造业。

[16] 规模以上服务业统计范围包括：年营业收入2000万元及以上的交通运输、仓储和邮政业，信息传输、软件和信息技术服务业，水利、环境和公共设施管理业，卫生行业法人单位；年营业收入1000万元及以上的房地产业（不含房地产开发经营），租赁和商务服务业，科学研究和技术服务业，教育行业法人单位；以及年营业收入500万元及以上的居民服务、修理和其他服务业，文化、体育和娱乐业，社会工作行业法人单位。

[17] 战略性新兴服务业包括新一代信息技术产业、高端装备制造产业、新材料产业、生物产业、新能源汽车产业、新能源产业、节能环保产业和数字创意产业等八大产业中的服务业相关行业，以及新技术与创新创业等相关服务业。2021年战略性新兴服务业企业营业收入增速按可比口径计算。

[18] 高技术产业投资包括医药制造、航空航天器及设备制造等六大类高技术制造业投资和信息服务、电子商务服务等九大类高技术服务业投资。

[19] 网上零售额是指通过公共网络交易平台（主要从事实物商品交易的网上平台，包括自建网站和第三方平台）实现的商品和服务零售额。

城乡区域协调发展扎实推进。年末全国常住人口城镇化率为64.72%，比上年末提高0.83个百分点。分区域看[20]，全年东部地区生产总值592202亿元，比上年增长8.1%；中部地区生产总值250132亿元，增长8.7%；西部地区生产总值239710亿元，增长7.4%；东北地区生产总值55699亿元，增长6.1%。全年京津冀地区生产总值96356亿元，比上年增长7.3%；长江经济带地区生产总值530228亿元，增长8.7%；长江三角洲地区生产总值276054亿元，增长8.4%。粤港澳大湾区建设、黄河流域生态保护和高质量发展等区域重大战略深入实施。

图7　2017-2021年年末常住人口城镇化率[21]

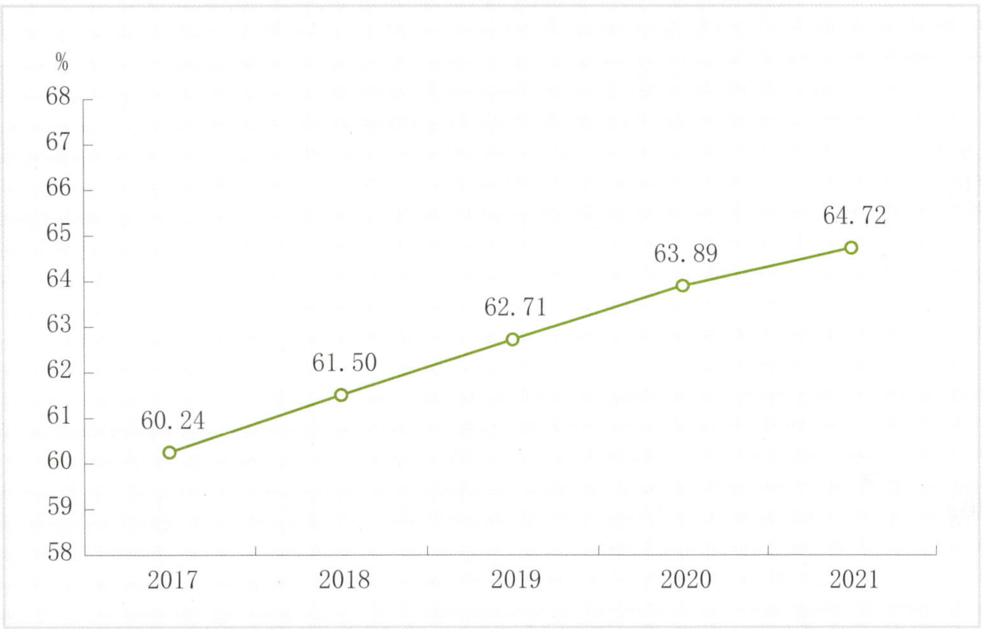

生态环境保护取得新成效。全年全国万元国内生产总值能耗[22]比上年下降2.7%。在监测的339个地级及以上城市中，全年空气质量达标的城市占64.3%，未达标的城市占35.7%；细颗粒物（$PM_{2.5}$）年平均浓度30微克/立方米，比上年下降9.1%。3641个国家地表水考核断面中，全年水质优良（Ⅰ～Ⅲ类）断面比例为84.9%，Ⅳ类断面比例为11.8%，Ⅴ类断面比例为2.2%，劣Ⅴ类断面比例为1.2%。

[20] 东部地区是指北京、天津、河北、上海、江苏、浙江、福建、山东、广东和海南10省（市）；中部地区是指山西、安徽、江西、河南、湖北和湖南6省；西部地区是指内蒙古、广西、重庆、四川、贵州、云南、西藏、陕西、甘肃、青海、宁夏和新疆12省（区、市）；东北地区是指辽宁、吉林和黑龙江3省。

[21] 根据第七次全国人口普查结果，对2017-2019年年末常住人口城镇化率数据进行了修订。

[22] 万元国内生产总值能耗按2020年价格计算。

二、农业

全年粮食种植面积11763万公顷，比上年增加86万公顷。其中，稻谷种植面积2992万公顷，减少15万公顷；小麦种植面积2357万公顷，增加19万公顷；玉米种植面积4332万公顷，增加206万公顷。棉花种植面积303万公顷，减少14万公顷。油料种植面积1310万公顷，减少3万公顷。糖料种植面积146万公顷，减少11万公顷。

全年粮食产量68285万吨，比上年增加1336万吨，增产2.0%。其中，夏粮产量14596万吨，增产2.2%；早稻产量2802万吨，增产2.7%；秋粮产量50888万吨，增产1.9%。全年谷物产量63276万吨，比上年增产2.6%。其中，稻谷产量21284万吨，增产0.5%；小麦产量13695万吨，增产2.0%；玉米产量27255万吨，增产4.6%。

图8 2017–2021年粮食产量

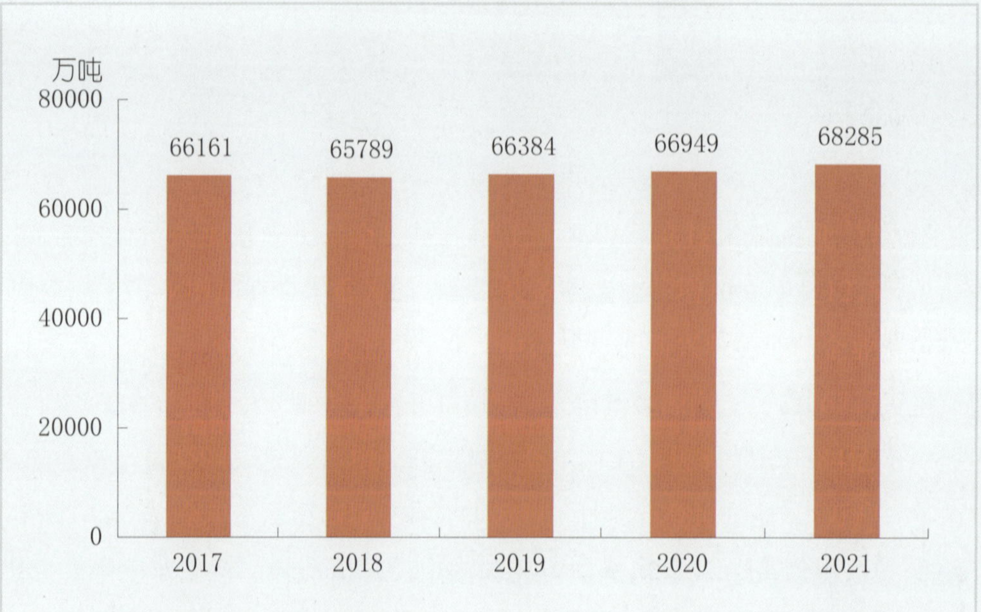

全年棉花产量573万吨，比上年减产3.0%。油料产量3613万吨，增产0.8%。糖料产量11451万吨，减产4.7%。茶叶产量318万吨，增产8.3%。

全年猪牛羊禽肉产量8887万吨，比上年增长16.3%。其中，猪肉产量5296万吨，增长28.8%；牛肉产量698万吨，增长3.7%；羊肉产量514万吨，增长4.4%；禽肉产量2380万吨，增长0.8%。禽蛋产量3409万吨，下降1.7%。牛奶产量3683万吨，增长7.1%。年末生猪存栏44922万头，比上年末增长10.5%；全年生猪出栏67128万头，比上年增长27.4%。

全年水产品产量6693万吨，比上年增长2.2%。其中，养殖水产品产量5388万吨，增长3.1%；捕捞水产品产量1305万吨，下降1.5%。

全年木材产量9888万立方米，比上年下降3.6%。

全年新增耕地灌溉面积46万公顷，新增高效节水灌溉面积188万公顷。

三、工业和建筑业

全年全部工业增加值372575亿元，比上年增长9.6%。规模以上工业增加值增长9.6%。在规模以上工业中，分经济类型看，国有控股企业增加值增长8.0%；股份制企业增长9.8%，外商及港澳台商投资企业增长8.9%；私营企业增长10.2%。分门类看，采矿业增长5.3%，制造业增长9.8%，电力、热力、燃气及水生产和供应业增长11.4%。

图 9　2017—2021 年全部工业增加值及其增长速度

全年规模以上工业中，农副食品加工业增加值比上年增长7.7%，纺织业增长1.4%，化学原料和化学制品制造业增长7.7%，非金属矿物制品业增长8.0%，黑色金属冶炼和压延加工业增长1.2%，通用设备制造业增长12.4%，专用设备制造业增长12.6%，汽车制造业增长5.5%，电气机械和器材制造业增长16.8%，计算机、通信和其他电子设备制造业增长15.7%，电力、热力生产和供应业增长10.9%。

表3 2021年主要工业产品产量及其增长速度[23]

产品名称	单位	产量	比上年增长（%）
纱	万吨	2873.7	9.8
布	亿米	502.0	9.3
化学纤维	万吨	6708.5	9.5
成品糖	万吨	1482.3	3.6
卷烟	亿支	24182.4	1.3
彩色电视机	万台	18496.5	-5.8
其中：液晶电视机	万台	17424.3	-9.5
家用电冰箱	万台	8992.1	-0.3
房间空气调节器	万台	21835.7	3.8
一次能源生产总量	亿吨标准煤	43.3	6.2
原煤	亿吨	41.3	5.7
原油	万吨	19888.1	2.1
天然气	亿立方米	2075.8	7.8
发电量	亿千瓦时	85342.5	9.7
其中：火电[24]	亿千瓦时	58058.7	8.9
水电	亿千瓦时	13390.0	-1.2
核电	亿千瓦时	4075.2	11.3
粗钢	万吨	103524.3	-2.8
钢材[25]	万吨	133666.8	0.9
十种有色金属	万吨	6477.1	4.7
其中：精炼铜（电解铜）	万吨	1048.7	4.6
原　铝（电解铝）	万吨	3850.3	3.8
水泥	亿吨	23.8	-0.4
硫酸（折100%）	万吨	9382.7	1.6
烧碱（折100%）	万吨	3891.3	5.9
乙烯	万吨	2825.7	30.8
化肥（折100%）	万吨	5543.6	0.9
发电机组（发电设备）	万千瓦	15954.6	19.2
汽车	万辆	2652.8	4.8
其中：基本型乘用车（轿车）	万辆	976.5	5.7
运动型多用途乘用车（SUV）	万辆	973.6	7.6
大中型拖拉机	万台	41.2	19.4
集成电路	亿块	3594.3	37.5
程控交换机	万线	699.6	-0.4
移动通信手持机	万台	166151.6	13.1
微型计算机设备	万台	46692.0	23.5
工业机器人	万台（套）	36.6	67.9

[23] 2020年部分产品产量数据进行了核实调整，2021年产量增速按可比口径计算。

[24] 火电包括燃煤发电量，燃油发电量，燃气发电量，余热、余压、余气发电量，垃圾焚烧发电量，生物质发电量。

[25] 钢材产量数据中含企业之间重复加工钢材。

年末全国发电装机容量237692万千瓦，比上年末增长7.9%。其中[26]，火电装机容量129678万千瓦，增长4.1%；水电装机容量39092万千瓦，增长5.6%；核电装机容量5326万千瓦，增长6.8%；并网风电装机容量32848万千瓦，增长16.6%；并网太阳能发电装机容量30656万千瓦，增长20.9%。

全年规模以上工业企业利润87092亿元，比上年增长[27]34.3%。分经济类型看，国有控股企业利润22770亿元，比上年增长56.0%；股份制企业62702亿元，增长40.2%，外商及港澳台商投资企业22846亿元，增长21.1%；私营企业29150亿元，增长27.6%。分门类看，采矿业利润10391亿元，比上年增长190.7%；制造业73612亿元，增长31.6%；电力、热力、燃气及水生产和供应业3089亿元，下降41.9%。全年规模以上工业企业每百元营业收入中的成本为83.74元，比上年减少0.23元；营业收入利润率为6.81%，提高0.76个百分点。年末规模以上工业企业资产负债率为56.1%，比上年末下降0.1个百分点。全年全国工业产能利用率[28]为77.5%。

全年建筑业增加值80138亿元，比上年增长2.1%。全国具有资质等级的总承包和专业承包建筑业企业利润8554亿元，比上年增长1.3%，其中国有控股企业3620亿元，增长8.0%。

图10　2017—2021年建筑业增加值及其增长速度

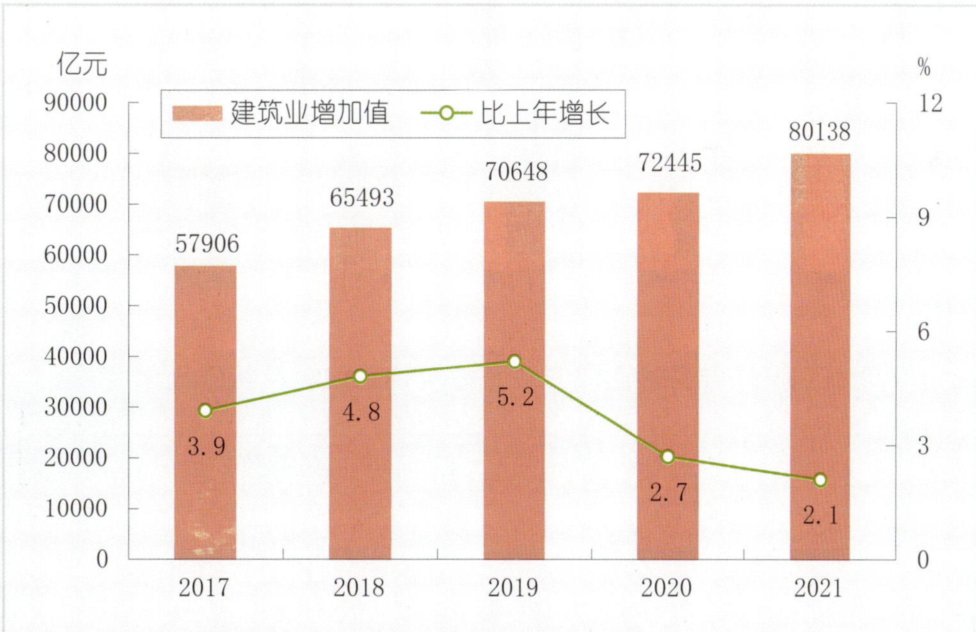

[26] 少量发电装机容量（如地热等）公报中未列出。

[27] 由于统计调查制度规定的调查范围变动、统计执法、剔除重复数据等因素，2021年规模以上工业企业财务指标增速及变化按可比口径计算。

[28] 产能利用率是指实际产出与生产能力（均以价值量计量）的比率。企业的实际产出是指企业报告期内的工业总产值；企业的生产能力是指报告期内，在劳动力、原材料、燃料、运输等保证供给的情况下，生产设备（机械）保持正常运行，企业可实现并能长期维持的产品产出。

四、服务业

全年批发和零售业增加值110493亿元，比上年增长11.3%；交通运输、仓储和邮政业增加值47061亿元，增长12.1%；住宿和餐饮业增加值17853亿元，增长14.5%；金融业增加值91206亿元，增长4.8%；房地产业增加值77561亿元，增长5.2%；信息传输、软件和信息技术服务业增加值43956亿元，增长17.2%；租赁和商务服务业增加值35350亿元，增长6.2%。全年规模以上服务业企业营业收入比上年增长18.7%，利润总额增长13.4%。

图11 2017—2021年服务业增加值及其增长速度

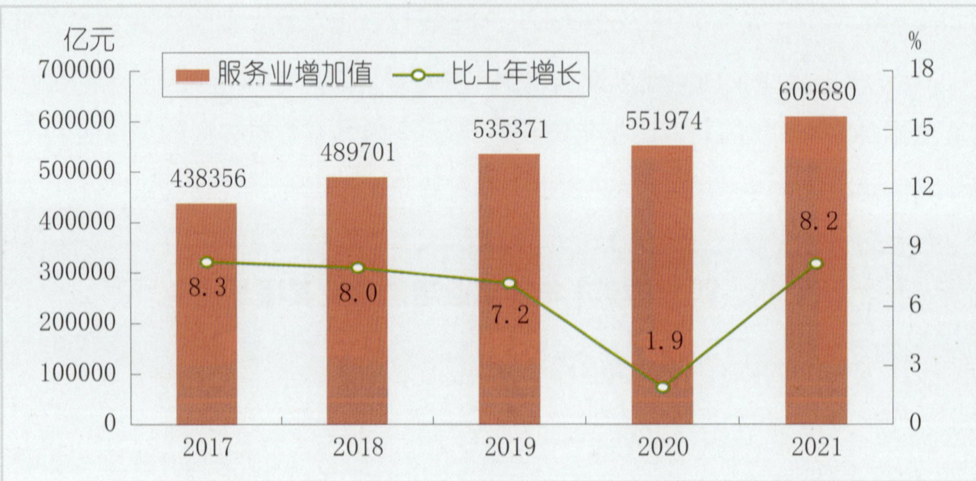

全年货物运输总量[29]530亿吨，货物运输周转量223574亿吨公里。全年港口完成货物吞吐量155亿吨，比上年增长6.8%，其中外贸货物吞吐量47亿吨，增长4.5%。港口集装箱吞吐量28272万标准箱，增长7.0%。

表4 2021年各种运输方式完成货物运输量及其增长速度

指 标	单 位	绝对数	比上年增长(%)
货物运输总量	**亿吨**	**529.7**	**12.3**
铁路	亿吨	47.2	5.9
公路	亿吨	391.4	14.2
水路	亿吨	82.4	8.2
民航	万吨	731.8	8.2
管道	亿吨	8.7	5.7
货物运输周转量	**亿吨公里**	**223574.4**	**13.7**
铁路	亿吨公里	33190.7	9.3
公路	亿吨公里	69087.7	14.8
水路	亿吨公里	115577.5	9.2
民航	亿吨公里	278.2	15.8
管道	亿吨公里	5440.3	4.9

[29]货物运输总量及周转量包括铁路、公路、水路、民航和管道五种运输方式完成量，2021年增速按可比口径计算。

全年旅客运输总量83亿人次，比上年下降14.1%。旅客运输周转量19758亿人公里，增长2.6%。

表5　2021年各种运输方式完成旅客运输量及其增长速度

指　标	单　位	绝对数	比上年增长（%）
旅客运输总量	亿人次	83.0	-14.1
铁路	亿人次	26.1	18.5
公路	亿人次	50.9	-26.2
水路	亿人次	1.6	9.0
民航	亿人次	4.4	5.5
旅客运输周转量	亿人公里	19758.2	2.6
铁路	亿人公里	9567.8	15.7
公路	亿人公里	3627.5	-21.8
水路	亿人公里	33.1	0.4
民航	亿人公里	6529.7	3.5

年末全国民用汽车保有量30151万辆（包括三轮汽车和低速货车732万辆），比上年末增加2064万辆，其中私人汽车保有量26246万辆，增加1852万辆。民用轿车保有量16739万辆，增加1099万辆，其中私人轿车保有量15732万辆，增加1059万辆。

全年完成邮政行业业务总量[30]13698亿元，比上年增长25.1%。邮政业全年完成邮政函件业务10.9亿件，包裹业务0.2亿件，快递业务量1083.0亿件，快递业务收入10332亿元。全年完成电信业务总量[31]16960亿元，比上年增长27.8%。年末移动电话基站数[32]996万个，其中4G基站590万个，5G基站143万个。全国电话用户总数182353万户，其中移动电话用户164283万户。移动电话普及率为116.3部/百人。固定互联网宽带接入用户[33]53579万户，比上年末增加5224万户，其中固定互联网光纤宽带接入用户[34]50551万户，增加5136万户。蜂窝物联网终端用户[35]13.99亿户，增加2.64亿户。互联网上网人数10.32亿人，其中手机上网人数[36]10.29亿人。互联网普及率为73.0%，其中农村地区互联网普及率为57.6%。全年移动互联网用户接入流量2216亿GB，比上年增长33.9%。全年软件和信息技术服务业[37]完成软件业务收入94994亿元，按可比口径计算，比上年增长17.7%。

[30] 邮政行业业务总量按2020年价格计算。

[31] 电信业务总量按2020年价格计算。

[32] 移动电话基站数是指报告期末为小区服务的无线收发信设备，处理基站与移动台之间的无线通信，在移动交换机与移动台之间起中继作用，监视无线传输质量的全套设备数。

[33] 固定互联网宽带接入用户是指报告期末在电信企业登记注册，通过xDSL、FTTx+LAN、FTTH/O以及其他宽带接入方式和普通专线接入公众互联网的用户。

[34] 固定互联网光纤宽带接入用户是指报告期末在电信企业登记注册，通过FTTH或FTTO方式接入公众互联网的用户。

[35] 蜂窝物联网终端用户是指报告期末接入移动通信网络并开通物联网业务的用户。物联网终端即连接传感网络层和传输网络层，实现远程采集数据及向网络层发送数据的物联网设备。

[36] 手机上网人数是指过去半年通过手机接入并使用互联网的人数。

[37] 软件和信息技术服务业包括软件开发、集成电路设计、信息系统集成和物联网技术服务、运行维护服务、信息处理和存储支持服务、信息技术咨询服务、数字内容服务和其他信息技术服务等行业。

图12 2017-2021年快递业务量及其增长速度

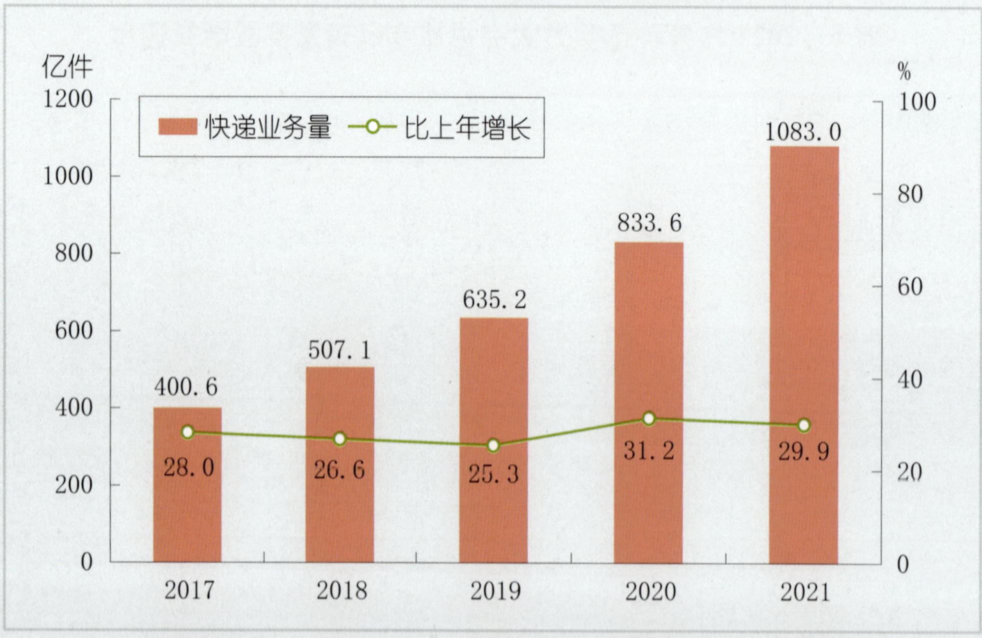

图13 2017-2021年年末固定互联网宽带接入用户数

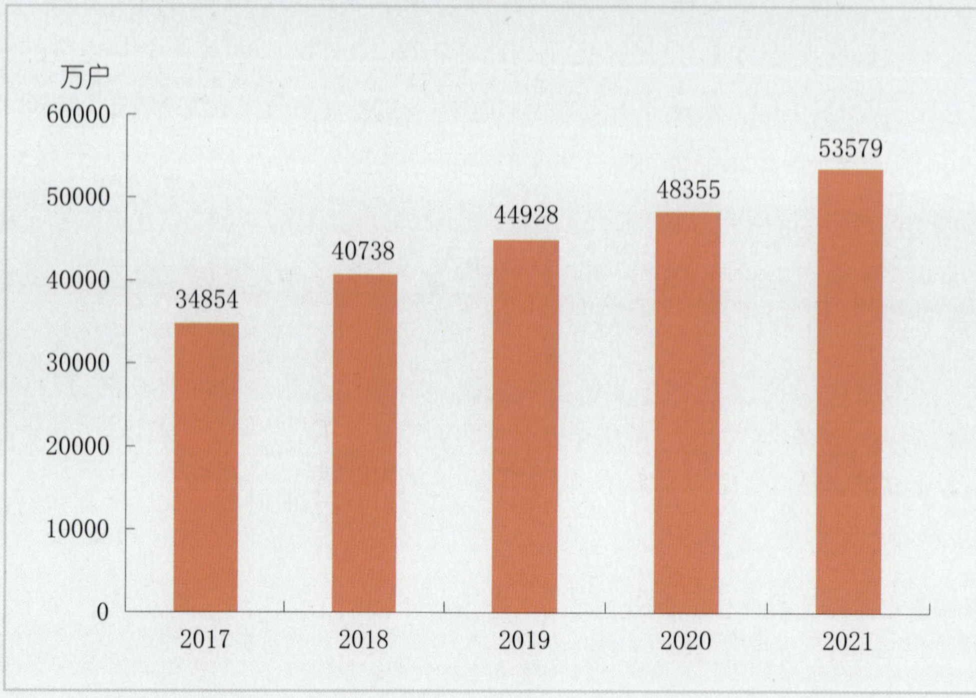

五、国内贸易

全年社会消费品零售总额440823亿元，比上年增长12.5%。按经营地统计，城镇消费品零售额381558亿元，增长12.5%；乡村消费品零售额59265亿元，增长12.1%。按消费类型统计，商品零售额393928亿元，增长11.8%；餐饮收入额46895亿元，增长18.6%。

图 14　2017-2021 年社会消费品零售总额及其增长速度

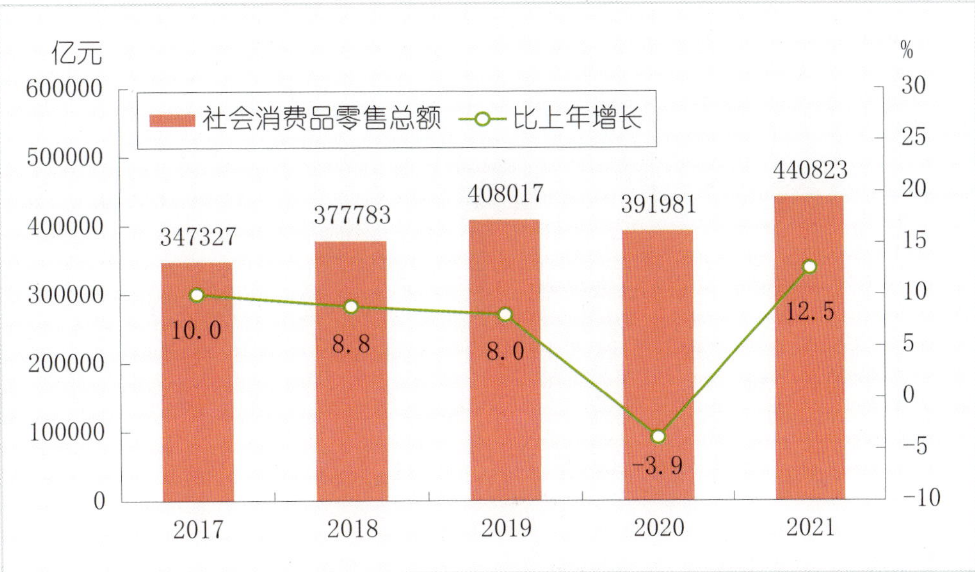

全年限额以上单位商品零售额中，粮油、食品类零售额比上年增长10.8%，饮料类增长20.4%，烟酒类增长21.2%，服装、鞋帽、针纺织品类增长12.7%，化妆品类增长14.0%，金银珠宝类增长29.8%，日用品类增长14.4%，家用电器和音像器材类增长10.0%，中西药品类增长9.9%，文化办公用品类增长18.8%，家具类增长14.5%，通讯器材类增长14.6%，建筑及装潢材料类增长20.4%，石油及制品类增长21.2%，汽车类增长7.6%。

全年实物商品网上零售额108042亿元，按可比口径计算，比上年增长12.0%，占社会消费品零售总额的比重为24.5%。

六、固定资产投资

全年全社会固定资产投资[38]552884亿元，比上年增长4.9%。固定资产投资（不含农户）544547亿元，增长4.9%。在固定资产投资（不含农户）中，分区域看[39]，东部地区投资增长6.4%，中部地区投资增长10.2%，西部地区投资增长3.9%，东北地区投资增长5.7%。

在固定资产投资（不含农户）中，第一产业投资14275亿元，比上年增长9.1%；第二产业投资167395亿元，增长11.3%；第三产业投资362877亿元，增长2.1%。民间固定资产投资[40]307659亿元，增长7.0%。基础设施投资[41]增长0.4%。社会领域投资[42]增长10.7%。

[38] 根据统计调查方法改革和制度规定，对 2020 年固定资产投资相关数据进行修订，2021 年相关指标增速按可比口径计算。

[39] 见注释 [20]。

[40] 民间固定资产投资是指具有集体、私营、个人性质的内资调查单位以及由其控股（包括绝对控股和相对控股）的调查单位建造或购置固定资产的投资。

[41] 基础设施投资包括交通运输、邮政业，电信、广播电视和卫星传输服务业，互联网和相关服务业，水利、环境和公共设施管理业投资。

[42] 社会领域投资包括教育，卫生和社会工作，文化、体育和娱乐业投资。

图15　2021年三次产业投资占固定资产投资（不含农户）比重

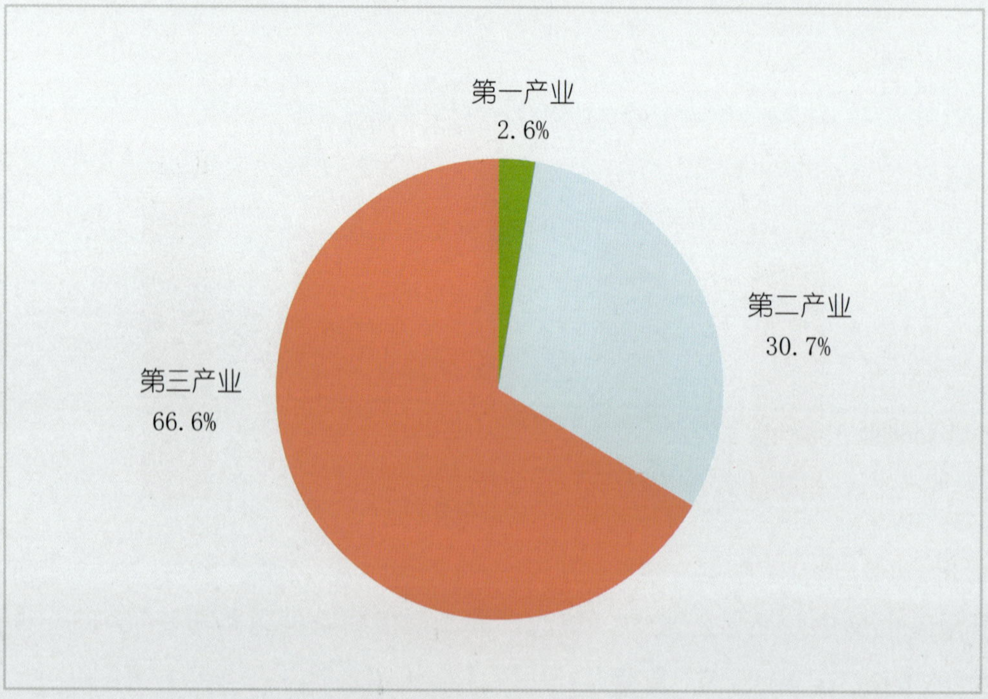

表6　2021年分行业固定资产投资（不含农户）增长速度

行　业	比上年增长（%）	行　业	比上年增长（%）
总　计	4.9	金融业	1.9
农、林、牧、渔业	9.3	房地产业[43]	5.0
采矿业	10.9	租赁和商务服务业	13.6
制造业	13.5	科学研究和技术服务业	14.5
电力、热力、燃气及水生产和供应业	1.1	水利、环境和公共设施管理业	-1.2
建筑业	1.6	居民服务、修理和其他服务业	-10.3
批发和零售业	-5.9	教育	11.7
交通运输、仓储和邮政业	1.6	卫生和社会工作	19.5
住宿和餐饮业	6.6	文化、体育和娱乐业	1.6
信息传输、软件和信息技术服务业	-12.1	公共管理、社会保障和社会组织	-38.2

[43]房地产业投资除房地产开发投资外，还包括建设单位自建房屋以及物业管理、中介服务和其他房地产投资。

表 7　2021 年固定资产投资新增主要生产与运营能力

指　标	单　位	绝对数
新增 220 千伏及以上变电设备	万千伏安	24334
新建铁路投产里程	公里	4208
其中：高速铁路	公里	2168
增、新建铁路复线投产里程	公里	2769
电气化铁路投产里程	公里	4189
新改建高速公路里程	公里	9028
港口万吨级码头泊位新增通过能力	万吨 / 年	25368
新增民用运输机场	个	7
新增光缆线路长度	万公里	319

全年房地产开发投资147602亿元，比上年增长4.4%。其中住宅投资111173亿元，增长6.4%；办公楼投资5974亿元，下降8.0%；商业营业用房投资12445亿元，下降4.8%。年末商品房待售面积51023万平方米，比上年末增加1173万平方米，其中商品住宅待售面积22761万平方米，增加381万平方米。

全年全国各类棚户区改造开工165万套，基本建成205万套；全国保障性租赁住房开工建设和筹集94万套。

表 8　2021 年房地产开发和销售主要指标及其增长速度

指　标	单　位	绝对数	比上年增长（%）
投资额	亿元	147602	4.4
其中：住宅	亿元	111173	6.4
房屋施工面积	万平方米	975387	5.2
其中：住宅	万平方米	690319	5.3
房屋新开工面积	万平方米	198895	-11.4
其中：住宅	万平方米	146379	-10.9
房屋竣工面积	万平方米	101412	11.2
其中：住宅	万平方米	73016	10.8
商品房销售面积	万平方米	179433	1.9
其中：住宅	万平方米	156532	1.1
本年到位资金	亿元	201132	4.2
其中：国内贷款	亿元	23296	-12.7
个人按揭贷款	亿元	32388	8.0

七、对外经济

全年货物进出口总额391009亿元，比上年增长21.4%。其中，出口217348亿元，增长21.2%；进口173661亿元，增长21.5%。货物进出口顺差43687亿元，比上年增加7344亿元。对“一带一路”[44]沿线国家进出口总额115979亿元，比上年增长23.6%。其中，出口65924亿元，增长21.5%；进口50055亿元，增长26.4%。

图16 2017—2021年货物进出口总额

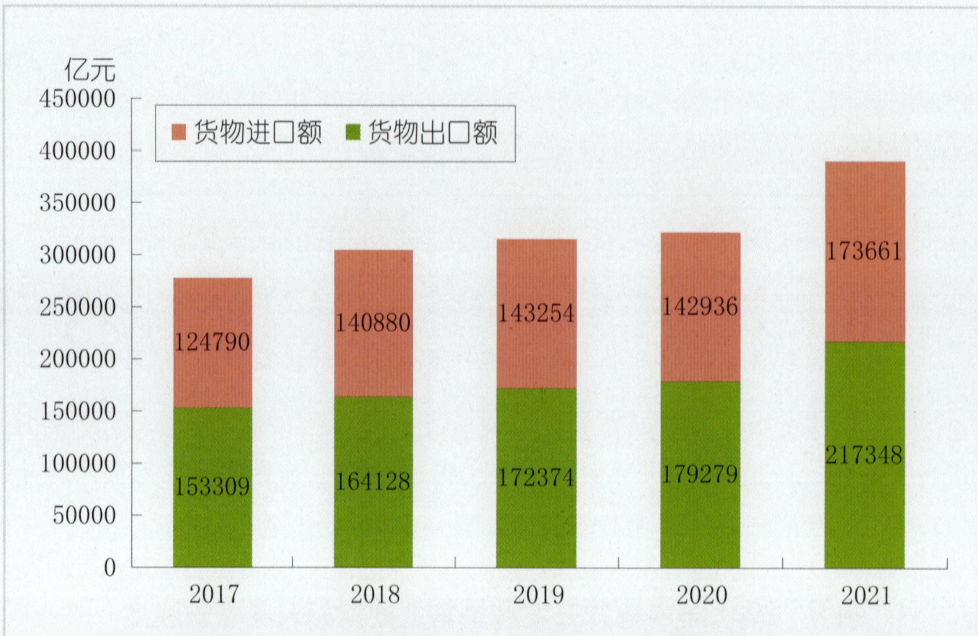

表9 2021年货物进出口总额及其增长速度

指　标	金额（亿元）	比上年增长（%）
货物进出口总额	**391009**	**21.4**
货物出口额	217348	21.2
其中：一般贸易	132445	24.4
加工贸易	53378	9.9
其中：机电产品	128286	20.4
高新技术产品	63266	17.9
货物进口额	173661	21.5
其中：一般贸易	108395	25.0
加工贸易	31601	13.3
其中：机电产品	73657	12.2
高新技术产品	54088	14.7
货物进出口顺差	**43687**	**20.2**

[44]“一带一路”是指“丝绸之路经济带”和“21世纪海上丝绸之路”。

表 10 2021 年主要商品出口数量、金额及其增长速度

商品名称	单 位	数 量	比上年增长（%）	金 额（亿元）	比上年增长（%）
钢材	万吨	6690	24.6	5289	67.9
纺织纱线、织物及制品	—	—	—	9384	-12.2
服装及衣着附件	—	—	—	11000	15.6
鞋靴	万双	873231	18.1	3097	26.2
家具及其零件	—	—	—	4772	18.2
箱包及类似容器	万吨	244	21.4	1800	26.1
玩具	—	—	—	2980	28.6
塑料制品	—	—	—	6397	20.5
集成电路	亿个	3107	19.6	9930	23.4
自动数据处理设备及其零部件	—	—	—	16488	12.9
手机	万台	95420	-1.2	9447	9.3
集装箱	万个	484	144.0	1514	198.3
液晶显示板	万个	142439	12.4	1788	30.5
汽车（包括底盘）	万辆	212	95.9	2227	104.6

表 11 2021 年主要商品进口数量、金额及其增长速度

商品名称	单 位	数 量	比上年增长（%）	金 额（亿元）	比上年增长（%）
大豆	万吨	9652	-3.8	3459	26.1
食用植物油	万吨	1039	-3.7	706	24.0
铁矿砂及其精矿	万吨	112432	-3.9	11942	39.6
煤及褐煤	万吨	32322	6.6	2319	64.1
原油	万吨	51298	-5.4	16618	34.4
成品油	万吨	2712	-4.0	1078	31.6
天然气	万吨	12136	19.9	3601	56.3
初级形状的塑料	万吨	3397	-16.4	3950	8.8
纸浆	万吨	2969	-2.7	1296	19.5
钢材	万吨	1427	-29.5	1210	3.9
未锻轧铜及铜材	万吨	553	-17.2	3387	12.5
集成电路	亿个	6355	16.9	27935	15.4
汽车（包括底盘）	万辆	94	0.6	3489	7.6

表12 2021年对主要国家和地区货物进出口金额、增长速度及其比重

国家和地区	出口额（亿元）	比上年增长（%）	占全部出口比重（%）	进口额（亿元）	比上年增长（%）	占全部进口比重（%）
东盟	31255	17.7	14.4	25489	22.2	14.7
欧盟	33483	23.7	15.4	20028	12.1	11.5
美国	37224	19.0	17.1	11603	24.2	6.7
日本	10722	8.5	4.9	13298	10.1	7.7
韩国	9617	23.5	4.4	13791	15.1	7.9
中国香港	22641	20.3	10.4	627	30.2	0.4
中国台湾	5063	21.7	2.3	16146	16.5	9.3
巴西	3464	43.4	1.6	7138	20.3	4.1
俄罗斯	4364	24.7	2.0	5122	28.2	2.9
印度	6302	36.6	2.9	1819	25.1	1.0
南非	1365	29.4	0.6	2147	49.4	1.2

全年服务进出口总额52983亿元，比上年增长16.1%。其中，服务出口25435亿元，增长31.4%；服务进口27548亿元，增长4.8%。服务进出口逆差2113亿元。

全年外商直接投资（不含银行、证券、保险领域）新设立企业47643家，比上年增长23.5%。实际使用外商直接投资金额11494亿元，增长14.9%，折1735亿美元，增长20.2%。其中“一带一路”沿线国家对华直接投资（含通过部分自由港对华投资）新设立企业5336家，增长24.3%；对华直接投资金额743亿元，增长29.4%，折112亿美元，增长36.0%。全年高技术产业实际使用外资3469亿元，增长17.1%，折522亿美元，增长22.1%。

表13 2021年外商直接投资（不含银行、证券、保险领域）及其增长速度

行业	企业数（家）	比上年增长（%）	实际使用金额（亿元）	比上年增长（%）
总计	**47643**	**23.5**	**11494**	**14.9**
其中：农、林、牧、渔业	491	-0.4	55	38.4
制造业	4455	19.4	2216	2.8
电力、热力、燃气及水生产和供应业	465	78.9	249	14.9
交通运输、仓储和邮政业	693	17.1	351	1.3
信息传输、软件和信息技术服务业	4053	15.1	1345	18.8
批发和零售业	13379	23.7	1098	34.1
房地产业	1125	-5.5	1571	11.7
租赁和商务服务业	9290	23.7	2193	19.3
居民服务、修理和其他服务业	522	16.8	31	44.6

全年对外非金融类直接投资额7332亿元，比上年下降3.5%，折1136亿美元，增长3.2%。其中，对“一带一路”沿线国家非金融类直接投资额203亿美元，增长14.1%。

表 14　2021 年对外非金融类直接投资额及其增长速度

行　业	金额（亿美元）	比上年增长（%）
总　计	1136.4	3.2
其中：农、林、牧、渔业	11.3	-18.7
采矿业	49.8	-2.2
制造业	184.0	-7.9
电力、热力、燃气及水生产和供应业	48.9	75.9
建筑业	55.7	7.9
批发和零售业	176.5	9.8
交通运输、仓储和邮政业	51.0	92.5
信息传输、软件和信息技术服务业	75.3	12.2
房地产业	24.9	-8.8
租赁和商务服务业	366.2	-12.4

全年对外承包工程完成营业额9996亿元，比上年下降7.1%，折1549亿美元，下降0.6%。其中，对“一带一路”沿线国家完成营业额897亿美元，下降1.6%，占对外承包工程完成营业额比重为57.9%。对外劳务合作派出各类劳务人员32万人。

八、财政金融

全年全国一般公共预算收入202539亿元，比上年增长10.7%，其中税收收入172731亿元，增长11.9%。全国一般公共预算支出246322亿元，比上年增长0.3%。全年新增减税降费约1.1万亿元。

图 17　2017—2021 年全国一般公共预算收入

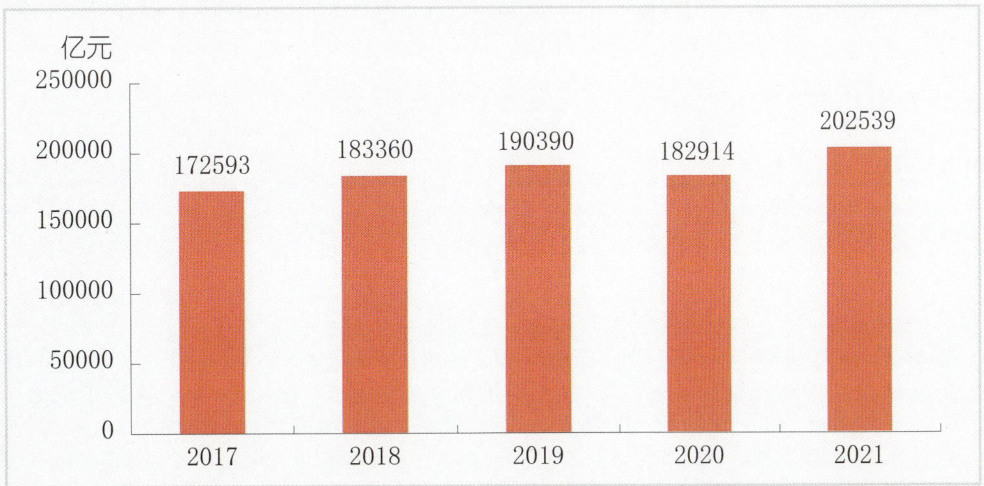

注：图中 2017 年至 2020 年数据为全国一般公共预算收入决算数，2021 年为执行数。

年末广义货币供应量（M_2）余额238.3万亿元，比上年末增长9.0%；狭义货币供应量（M_1）余额64.7万亿元，增长3.5%；流通中货币（M_0）余额9.1万亿元，增长7.7%。

全年社会融资规模增量[45]31.4万亿元，按可比口径计算，比上年少3.4万亿元。年末社会融资规模存量[46]314.1万亿元，按可比口径计算，比上年末增长10.3%，其中对实体经济发放的人民币贷款余额191.5万亿元，增长11.6%。年末全部金融机构本外币各项存款余额238.6万亿元，比年初增加20.2万亿元，其中人民币各项存款余额232.3万亿元，增加19.7万亿元。全部金融机构本外币各项贷款余额198.5万亿元，增加20.1万亿元，其中人民币各项贷款余额192.7万亿元，增加19.9万亿元。人民币普惠金融贷款[47]余额26.5万亿元，增加5.0万亿元。

表15　2021年年末全部金融机构本外币存贷款余额及其增长速度

指　标	年末数（亿元）	比上年末增长（%）
各项存款	**2386062**	**9.3**
其中：境内住户存款	1033118	10.6
其中：人民币	1025012	10.7
境内非金融企业存款	730137	6.1
各项贷款	**1985108**	**11.3**
其中：境内短期贷款	520506	5.7
境内中长期贷款	1291149	13.5

年末主要农村金融机构（农村信用社、农村合作银行、农村商业银行）人民币贷款余额242496亿元，比年初增加26607亿元。全部金融机构人民币消费贷款余额548849亿元，增加53181亿元。其中，个人短期消费贷款余额93558亿元，增加6080亿元；个人中长期消费贷款余额455292亿元，增加47101亿元。

全年沪深交易所A股累计筹资[48]16743亿元，比上年增加1326亿元。沪深交易所首次公开发行上市A股481只，筹资5351亿元，比上年增加609亿元，其中科创板股票162只，筹资2029亿元；沪深

[45] 社会融资规模增量是指一定时期内实体经济从金融体系获得的资金总额。

[46] 社会融资规模存量是指一定时期末（月末、季末或年末）实体经济从金融体系获得的资金余额。

[47] 普惠金融贷款包括单户授信小于1000万元的小微型企业贷款、个体工商户经营性贷款、小微企业主经营性贷款、农户生产经营贷款、建档立卡贫困人口消费贷款、创业担保贷款和助学贷款。

[48] 沪深交易所股票筹资额按上市日统计，筹资额包括了可转债实际转股金额，2020年、2021年可转债实际转股金额分别为1195亿元、1342亿元。

交易所A股再融资（包括公开增发、定向增发、配股、优先股、可转债转股）11391亿元，增加717亿元。北京证券交易所公开发行股票11只，筹资[49]21亿元。全年各类主体通过沪深交易所发行债券（包括公司债、可转债、可交换债、政策性金融债、地方政府债和企业资产支持证券）筹资86553亿元，比上年增加1776亿元。全国中小企业股份转让系统[50]挂牌公司6932家，全年挂牌公司累计股票筹资260亿元。

全年发行公司信用类债券[51]14.7万亿元，比上年增加0.5万亿元。

全年保险公司原保险保费收入[52]44900亿元，按可比口径计算，比上年增长4.0%。其中，寿险业务原保险保费收入23572亿元，健康险和意外伤害险业务原保险保费收入9657亿元，财产险业务原保险保费收入11671亿元。支付各类赔款及给付15609亿元。其中，寿险业务给付3540亿元，健康险和意外伤害险业务赔款及给付4381亿元，财产险业务赔款7687亿元。

九、居民收入消费和社会保障

全年全国居民人均可支配收入35128元，比上年增长9.1%，扣除价格因素，实际增长8.1%。全国居民人均可支配收入中位数[53]29975元，增长8.8%。按常住地分，城镇居民人均可支配收入47412元，比上年增长8.2%，扣除价格因素，实际增长7.1%。城镇居民人均可支配收入中位数43504元，增长7.7%。农村居民人均可支配收入18931元，比上年增长10.5%，扣除价格因素，实际增长9.7%。农村居民人均可支配收入中位数16902元，增长11.2%。城乡居民人均可支配收入比值为2.50，比上年缩小0.06。按全国居民五等份收入分组[54]，低收入组人均可支配收入8333元，中间偏下收入组人均可支配收入18445元，中间收入组人均可支配收入29053元，中间偏上收入组人均可支配收入44949元，高收入组人均可支配收入85836元。全国农民工人均月收入4432元，比上年增长8.8%。全年脱贫县[55]农村居民人均可支配收入14051元，比上年增长11.6%，扣除价格因素，实际增长10.8%。

---

[49] 北京证券交易所股票筹资额按上市日统计，筹资额只计入北京证券交易所开市日起新上市公司，精选层平移公司历史筹资数据保留在原全国中小企业股份转让系统统计报表中。

[50] 全国中小企业股份转让系统是 2012 年经国务院批准的全国性证券交易场所。全年全国中小企业股份转让系统挂牌公司累计筹资不含优先股，股票筹资按新增股份挂牌日统计。

[51] 公司信用类债券包括非金融企业债务融资工具、企业债券以及公司债、可转债等。

[52] 原保险保费收入是指保险企业确认的原保险合同保费收入。

[53] 人均收入中位数是指将所有调查户按人均收入水平从低到高（或从高到低）顺序排列，处于最中间位置调查户的人均收入。

[54] 全国居民五等份收入分组是指将所有调查户按人均收入水平从低到高顺序排列，平均分为五个等份，处于最低 20% 的收入家庭为低收入组，依此类推依次为中间偏下收入组、中间收入组、中间偏上收入组、高收入组。

[55] 脱贫县包括原 832 个国家扶贫开发工作重点县和集中连片特困地区县，以及新疆阿克苏地区 7 个市县。

全年全国居民人均消费支出24100元，比上年增长13.6%，扣除价格因素，实际增长12.6%。其中，人均服务性消费支出[56]10645元，比上年增长17.8%，占居民人均消费支出的比重为44.2%。按常住地分，城镇居民人均消费支出30307元，增长12.2%，扣除价格因素，实际增长11.1%；农村居民人均消费支出15916元，增长16.1%，扣除价格因素，实际增长15.3%。全国居民恩格尔系数为29.8%，其中城镇为28.6%，农村为32.7%。

图 18　2017—2021 年全国居民人均可支配收入及其增长速度

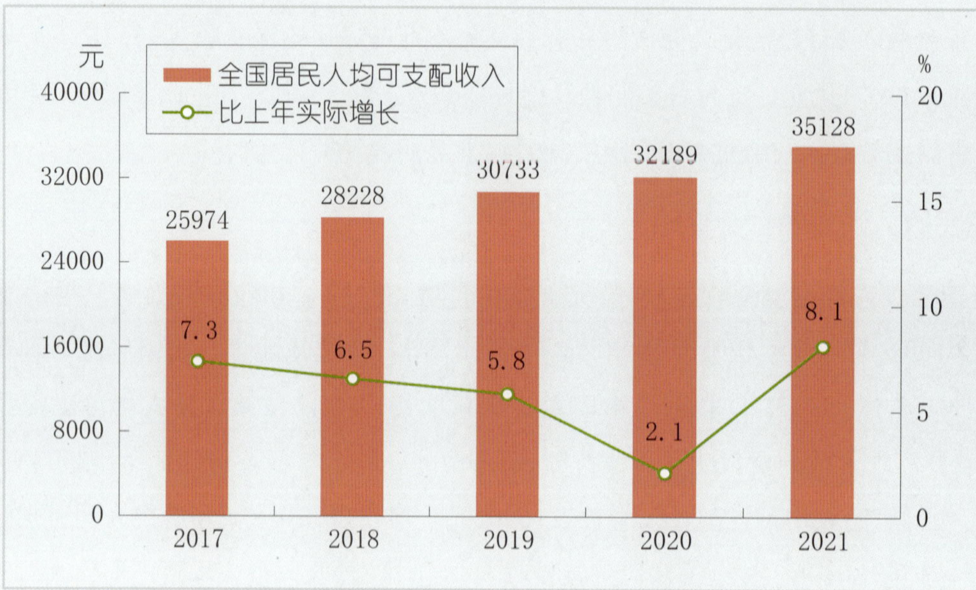

图 19　2021 年全国居民人均消费支出及其构成

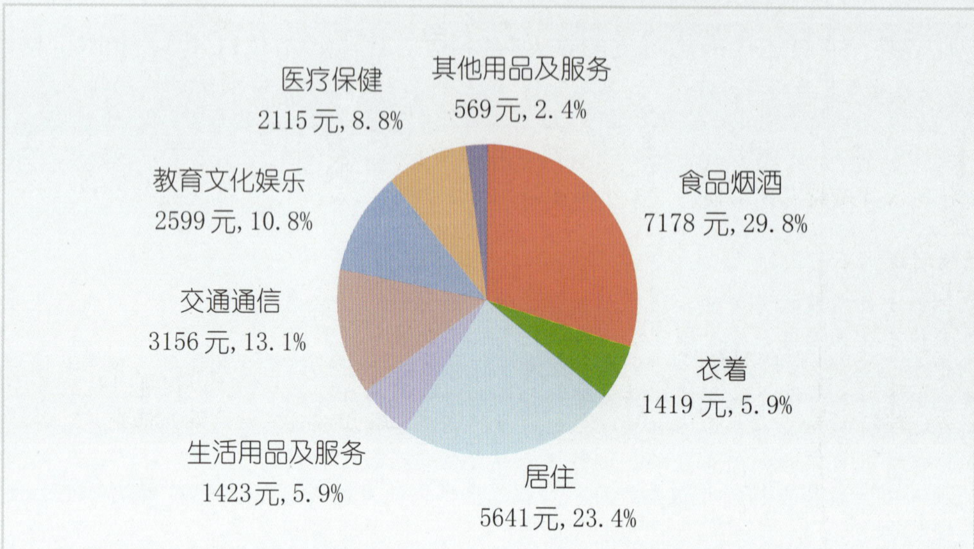

[56] 服务性消费支出是指住户用于餐饮服务、教育文化娱乐服务和医疗服务等各种生活服务的消费支出。

年末全国参加城镇职工基本养老保险人数48075万人，比上年末增加2454万人。参加城乡居民基本养老保险人数54797万人，增加554万人。参加基本医疗保险人数136424万人，增加293万人。其中，参加职工基本医疗保险人数35422万人，增加967万人；参加城乡居民基本医疗保险人数101002万人。参加失业保险人数22958万人，增加1268万人。年末全国领取失业保险金人数259万人。参加工伤保险人数28284万人，增加1521万人，其中参加工伤保险的农民工9086万人，增加152万人。参加生育保险人数23851万人，增加283万人。年末全国共有738万人享受城市最低生活保障，3474万人享受农村最低生活保障，438万人享受农村特困人员[57]救助供养，全年临时救助[58]1089万人次。全年国家抚恤、补助退役军人和其他优抚对象817万人。

年末全国共有各类提供住宿的民政服务机构4.3万个，其中养老机构4.0万个，儿童福利和救助保护机构801个。民政服务床位[59]840.2万张，其中养老服务床位813.5万张，儿童福利和救助保护机构床位9.6万张。年末共有社区服务中心2.9万个，社区服务站47.2万个。

十、科学技术和教育

全年研究与试验发展（R&D）经费支出27864亿元，比上年增长14.2%，与国内生产总值之比为2.44%，其中基础研究经费1696亿元。国家自然科学基金共资助4.87万个项目。截至年末，正在运行的国家重点实验室533个，纳入新序列管理的国家工程研究中心191个，国家企业技术中心1636家，大众创业万众创新示范基地212家。国家科技成果转化引导基金累计设立36支子基金，资金总规模624亿元。国家级科技企业孵化器[60]1287家，国家备案众创空间[61]2551家。全年授予专利权460.1万件，比上年增长26.4%；PCT专利申请受理量[62]7.3万件。截至年末，有效专利1542.1万件，其中境内有效发明专利270.4万件。每万人口高价值发明专利拥有量[63]7.5件。全年商标注册773.9万件，比上年增长34.3%。全年共签订技术合同67万项，技术合同成交金额37294亿元，比上年增长32.0%。

---

[57] 农村特困人员是指无劳动能力，无生活来源，无法定赡养、抚养、扶养义务人或者其法定义务人无履行义务能力的农村老年人、残疾人以及未满16周岁的未成年人。

[58] 临时救助是指国家对遭遇突发事件、意外伤害、重大疾病或其他特殊原因导致基本生活陷入困境，其他社会救助制度暂时无法覆盖或救助之后基本生活暂时仍有严重困难的家庭或个人给予的应急性、过渡性的救助。

[59] 民政服务床位除收养性机构外，还包括救助类机构、社区类机构的床位。

[60] 国家级科技企业孵化器是指符合《科技企业孵化器管理办法》规定的，以促进科技成果转化、培育科技企业和企业家精神为宗旨，提供物理空间、共享设施和专业化服务的科技创业服务机构，且经过科学技术部批准确定的科技企业孵化器。

[61] 国家备案众创空间是指符合《发展众创空间工作指引》规定的新型创新创业服务平台，且按照《国家众创空间备案暂行规定》经科学技术部审核备案的众创空间。

[62] PCT专利申请受理量是指国家知识产权局作为PCT专利申请受理局受理的PCT专利申请数量。PCT(Patent Cooperation Treaty)即专利合作条约，是专利领域的一项国际合作条约。

[63] 每万人口高价值发明专利拥有量是指每万人口本国居民拥有的经国家知识产权局授权的符合下列任一条件的有效发明专利数量：战略性新兴产业的发明专利；在海外有同族专利权的发明专利；维持年限超过10年的发明专利；实现较高质押融资金额的发明专利；获得国家科学技术奖、中国专利奖的发明专利。

图 20　2017–2021 年研究与试验发展（R&D）经费支出及其增长速度

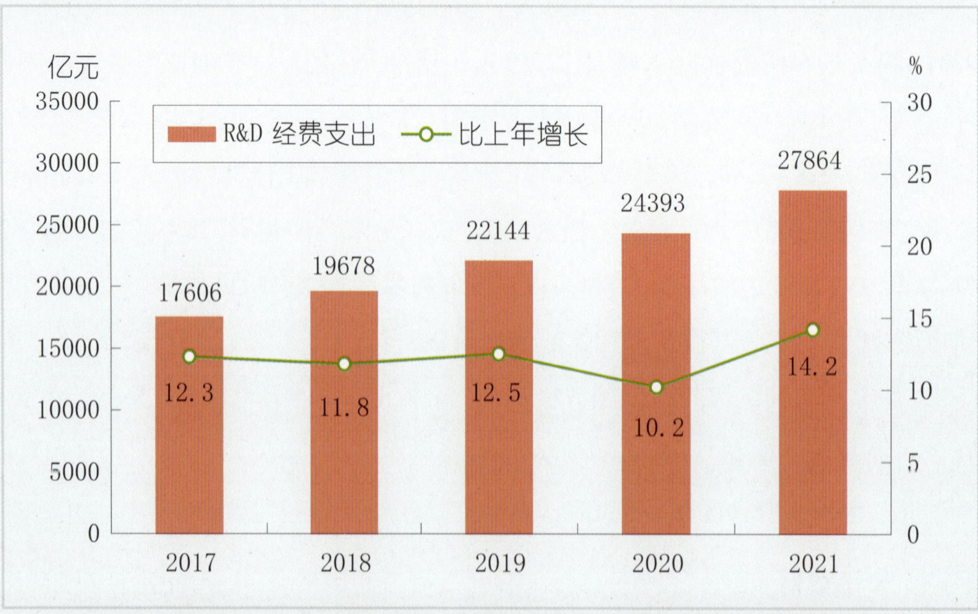

表 16　2021 年专利授权和有效专利情况

指　标	专利数（万件）	比上年增长（%）
专利授权数	**460.1**	**26.4**
其中：境内专利授权	445.1	27.0
其中：发明专利授权	69.6	31.3
其中：境内发明专利	57.8	33.2
年末有效专利数	**1542.1**	**26.5**
其中：境内有效专利	1429.5	28.6
其中：有效发明专利	359.7	17.6
其中：境内有效发明专利	270.4	22.2

全年成功完成52次宇航发射。天问一号探测器成功着陆火星，祝融号火星车驶上火星表面。天和核心舱发射成功，神舟十二号、神舟十三号等任务相继实施，中国人首次进入自己的空间站。羲和号探日卫星成功发射运行。祖冲之二号、九章二号成功研制，我国在超导量子和光量子两种物理体系上实现量子计算优越性。海斗一号全海深无人潜水器打破多项世界纪录。华龙一号自主三代核电机组投入商业运行。

年末全国共有国家质检中心869家。全国现有产品质量、体系和服务认证机构932个，累计完成对87万家企业的认证。全年制定、修订国家标准2815项，其中新制定1900项。全年制造业产品质量合格率[64]为93.08%。

全年研究生教育招生117.7万人，在学研究生333.2万人，毕业生77.3万人。普通、职业本专科[65]招生1001.3万人，在校生3496.1万人，毕业生826.5万人。中等职业教育[66]招生656.2万人，在校生1738.5万人，毕业生484.1万人。普通高中招生905.0万人，在校生2605.0万人，毕业生780.2万人。初中招生1705.4万人，在校生5018.4万人，毕业生1587.1万人。普通小学招生1782.6万人，在校生10779.9万人，毕业生1718.0万人。特殊教育招生14.9万人，在校生92.0万人，毕业生14.6万人。学前教育在园幼儿4805.2万人。九年义务教育巩固率为95.4%，高中阶段毛入学率为91.4%。

图21　2017–2021年本专科、中等职业教育及普通高中招生人数

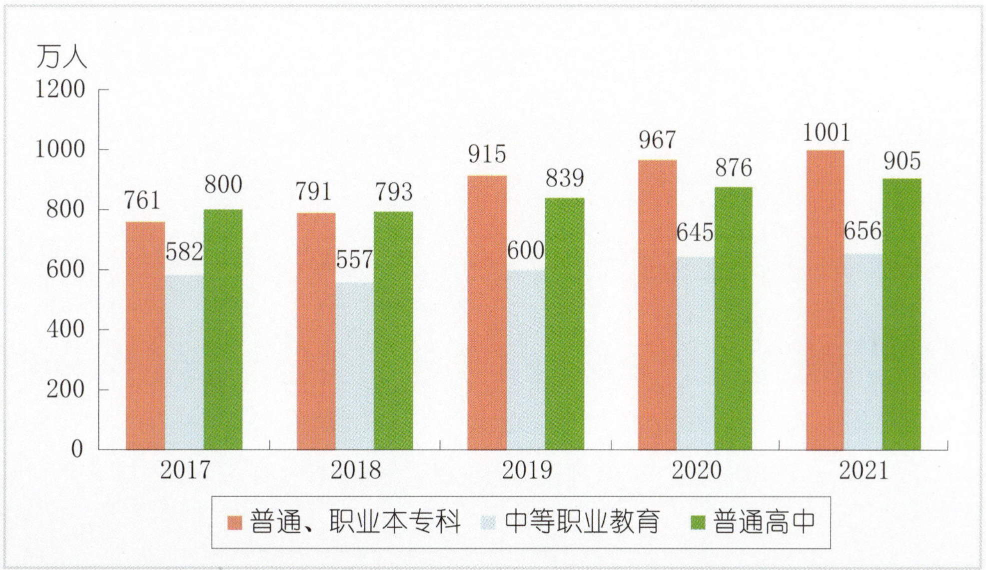

十一、文化旅游、卫生健康和体育

年末全国文化和旅游系统共有艺术表演团体2044个，博物馆3671个。全国共有公共图书馆3217个，总流通[67]72898万人次；文化馆3317个。有线电视实际用户2.01亿户，其中有线数字电视实际用户1.95亿户。年末广播节目综合人口覆盖率为99.5%，电视节目综合人口覆盖率为99.7%。全年

[64] 制造业产品质量合格率是指以产品质量检验为手段，按照规定的方法、程序和标准实施质量抽样检测，判定为质量合格的样品数占全部抽样样品数的百分比，统计调查样本覆盖制造业的29个行业。

[65] 普通、职业本专科包括普通本科、职业本科、高职（专科）。2021年高职（专科）招生人数统计口径发生变化，包含五年制高职转入专科招生人数。

[66] 中等职业教育包括普通中专、成人中专、职业高中和技工学校。

[67] 总流通人次是指本年度内到图书馆场馆接受图书馆服务的总人次，包括借阅书刊、咨询问题以及参加各类读者活动等。

生产电视剧194部6736集，电视动画片78372分钟。全年生产故事影片565部，科教、纪录、动画和特种影片[68]175部。出版各类报纸276亿份，各类期刊20亿册，图书110亿册（张），人均图书拥有量[69]7.76册（张）。年末全国共有档案馆4233个，已开放各类档案18931万卷（件）。全年全国规模以上文化及相关产业企业营业收入119064亿元，按可比口径计算，比上年增长16.0%。

全年国内游客32.5亿人次，比上年增长12.8%。其中，城镇居民游客23.4亿人次，增长13.4%；农村居民游客9.0亿人次，增长11.1%。国内旅游收入29191亿元，增长31.0%。其中，城镇居民游客花费23644亿元，增长31.6%；农村居民游客花费5547亿元，增长28.4%。

图 22　2017—2021 年国内游客人次及其增长速度

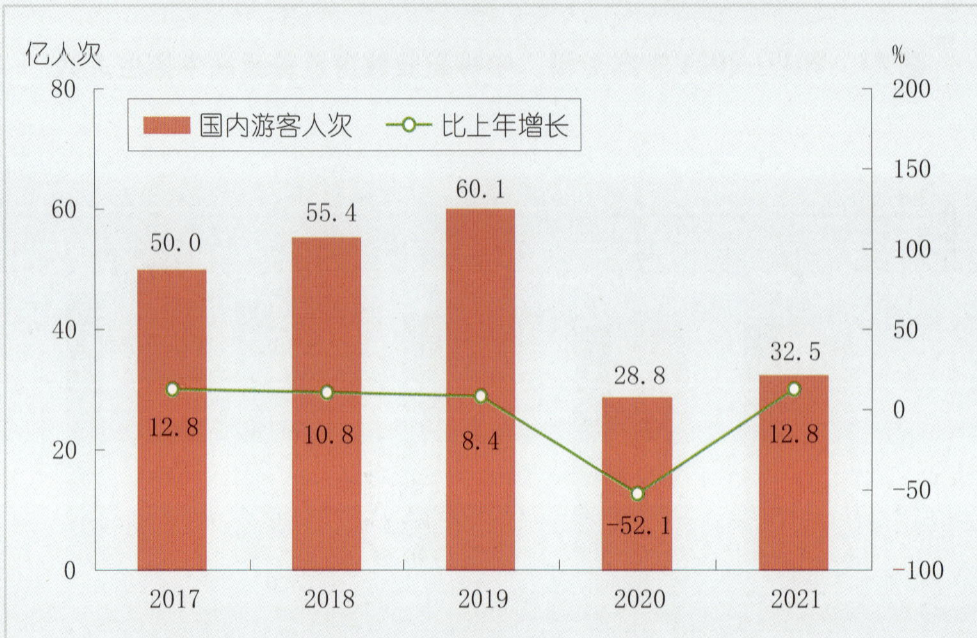

年末全国共有医疗卫生机构103.1万个，其中医院3.7万个，在医院中有公立医院1.2万个，民营医院2.5万个；基层医疗卫生机构97.7万个，其中乡镇卫生院3.5万个，社区卫生服务中心（站）3.6万个，门诊部（所）30.7万个，村卫生室59.9万个；专业公共卫生机构1.3万个，其中疾病预防控制中心3380个，卫生监督所（中心）2790个。年末卫生技术人员1123万人，其中执业医师和执业助理医师427万人，注册护士502万人。医疗卫生机构床位957万张，其中医院748万张，乡镇卫生院144万张。全年总诊疗人次[70]85.3亿人次，出院人数[71]2.4亿人。截至年末，全国累计报告新型冠状

[68] 特种影片是指采用与常规影院放映在技术、设备、节目方面不同的电影展示方式，如巨幕电影、立体电影、立体特效（4D）电影、动感电影、球幕电影等。

[69] 人均图书拥有量是指在一年内全国平均每人能拥有的当年出版图书册数。

[70] 总诊疗人次是指所有诊疗工作的总人次数，包括门诊、急诊、出诊、预约诊疗、单项健康检查、健康咨询指导（不含健康讲座、核酸检测）人次。

[71] 出院人数是指报告期内所有住院后出院的人数，包括医嘱离院、医嘱转其他医疗机构、非医嘱离院、死亡及其他人数，不含家庭病床撤床人数。

病毒肺炎确诊病例102314例，累计治愈出院病例94792例，累计死亡4636人。全国累计报告接种新型冠状病毒疫苗283533万剂次。全国共有11937家医疗卫生机构提供新型冠状病毒核酸检测服务，总检测能力达到4168万份/天。

图23　2017-2021年年末卫生技术人员人数

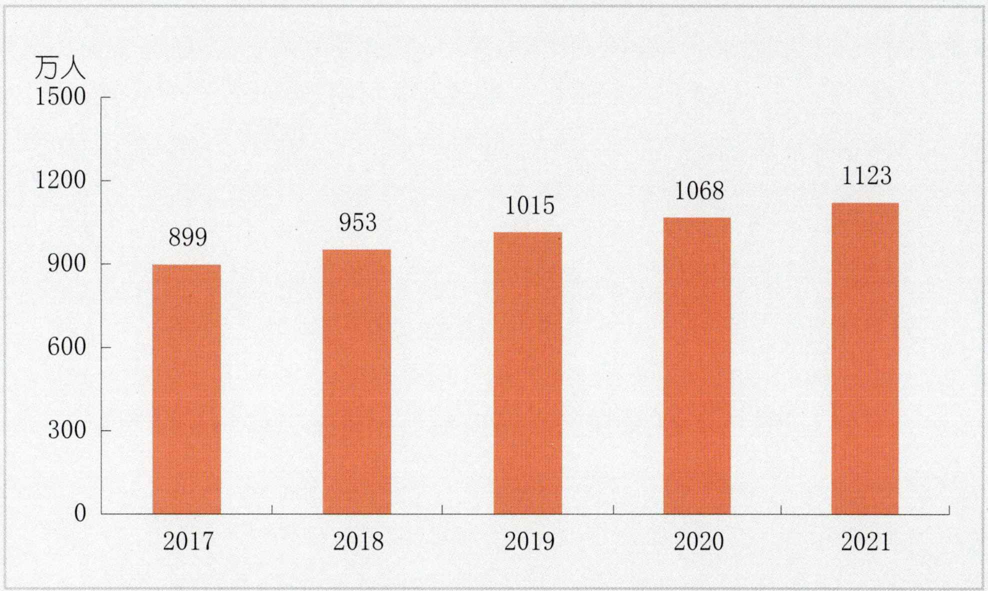

年末全国共有体育场地[72]397.1万个，体育场地面积[73]34.1亿平方米，人均体育场地面积2.41平方米。全年我国运动员在16个运动大项中获得67个世界冠军，共创12项世界纪录。在第32届奥运会上，我国运动员共获得38枚金牌，奖牌总数88枚，位列奥运会金牌榜和奖牌榜第二位。全年我国残疾人运动员在5项国际赛事中获得110个世界冠军。在第16届残奥会上，我国运动员共获得96枚金牌，奖牌总数207枚，第五次蝉联金牌榜和奖牌榜第一位。

十二、资源、环境和应急管理

全年全国国有建设用地供应总量[74]69.0万公顷，比上年增长4.8%。其中，工矿仓储用地17.5万公顷，增长4.9%；房地产用地[75]13.6万公顷，减少12.2%；基础设施用地37.9万公顷，增长12.7%。

全年水资源总量29520亿立方米。全年总用水量5921亿立方米，比上年增长1.9%。其中，生活用水增长5.3%，工业用水增长2.0%，农业用水增长0.9%，人工生态环境补水增长2.9%。万元国内

[72] 体育场地调查对象不包括军队、铁路系统所属体育场地。
[73] 体育场地面积是指体育训练、比赛、健身场地的有效面积。
[74] 国有建设用地供应总量是指报告期内市、县人民政府根据年度土地供应计划依法以出让、划拨、租赁等方式与用地单位或个人签订出让合同或签发划拨决定书、完成交易的国有建设用地总量。
[75] 房地产用地是指商服用地和住宅用地的总和。

生产总值用水量[76]54立方米，下降5.8%。万元工业增加值用水量31立方米，下降7.0%。人均用水量419立方米，增长1.8%。

全年完成造林面积360万公顷，其中人工造林面积134万公顷，占全部造林面积的37.1%。种草改良面积[77]307万公顷。截至年末，国家级自然保护区474个，国家公园5个。新增水土流失治理面积6.2万平方公里。

初步核算，全年能源消费总量52.4亿吨标准煤，比上年增长5.2%。煤炭消费量增长4.6%，原油消费量增长4.1%，天然气消费量增长12.5%，电力消费量增长10.3%。煤炭消费量占能源消费总量的56.0%，比上年下降0.9个百分点；天然气、水电、核电、风电、太阳能发电等清洁能源消费量占能源消费总量的25.5%，上升1.2个百分点。重点耗能工业企业单位电石综合能耗下降5.3%，单位合成氨综合能耗与上年持平，吨钢综合能耗下降0.4%，单位电解铝综合能耗下降2.1%，每千瓦时火力发电标准煤耗下降0.5%。全国万元国内生产总值二氧化碳排放[78]下降3.8%。

图24 2017–2021年清洁能源消费量占能源消费总量的比重

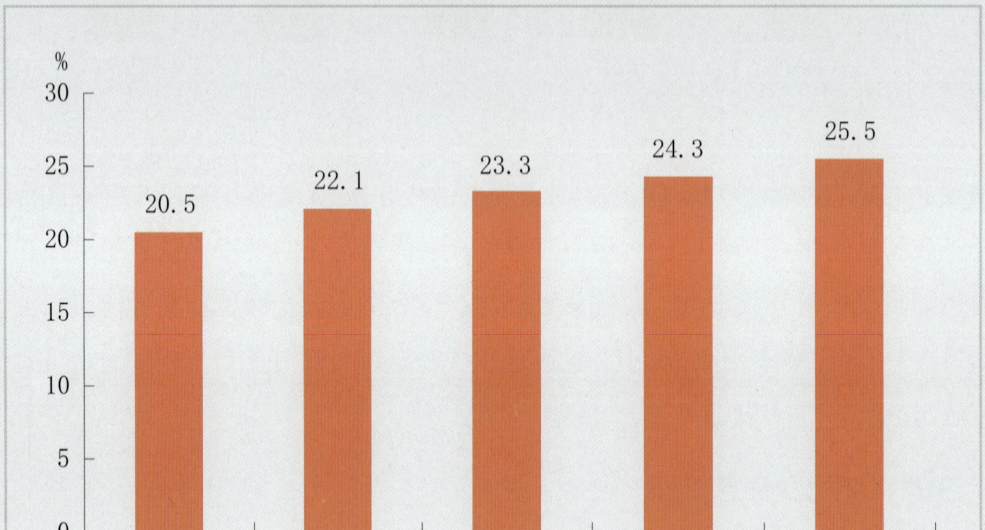

全年近岸海域海水水质[79]达到国家一、二类海水水质标准的面积占81.3%，三类海水占5.2%，四类、劣四类海水占13.5%。

---

[76] 万元国内生产总值用水量、万元工业增加值用水量按2020年价格计算。

[77] 种草改良面积是指通过实施播种、栽种等措施增加牧草数量的面积以及通过压盐压碱压沙、土壤改良、围栏封育等措施使草原原生植被、生态得到改善的面积之和。

[78] 万元国内生产总值二氧化碳排放按2020年价格计算。

[79] 近岸海域海水水质采用面积法进行评价。

在开展城市区域声环境监测的324个城市中，全年昼间声环境质量好的城市占4.9%，较好的占61.7%，一般的占31.5%，较差的占1.9%。

全年平均气温为10.53℃，比上年上升0.28℃。共有5个台风登陆。

全年农作物受灾面积1174万公顷，其中绝收163万公顷。全年因洪涝和地质灾害造成直接经济损失2477亿元，因干旱灾害造成直接经济损失201亿元，因低温冷冻和雪灾造成直接经济损失133亿元，因海洋灾害造成直接经济损失30亿元。全年大陆地区共发生5.0级以上地震20次，造成直接经济损失107亿元。全年共发生森林火灾616起，受害森林面积约0.4万公顷。

全年各类生产安全事故共死亡26307人。工矿商贸企业就业人员10万人生产安全事故死亡人数1.374人，比上年上升5.6%；煤矿百万吨死亡人数0.045人，下降23.7%。道路交通事故万车死亡人数1.57人，下降5.4%。

资料来源：

本公报中城镇新增就业、城镇登记失业率、养老保险、失业保险、工伤保险、技工学校数据来自人力资源和社会保障部；外汇储备、汇率数据来自国家外汇管理局；市场主体、质量检验、国家标准制定修订、制造业产品质量合格率数据来自国家市场监督管理总局；环境监测等数据来自生态环境部；水产品产量、新增高效节水灌溉面积数据来自农业农村部；木材产量、造林面积、种草改良面积、国家级自然保护区、国家公园数据来自国家林业和草原局；新增耕地灌溉面积、水资源总量、用水量、新增水土流失治理面积数据来自水利部；发电装机容量、新增220千伏及以上变电设备、电力消费量数据来自中国电力企业联合会；港口货物吞吐量、港口集装箱吞吐量、公路运输、水路运输、新改建高速公路里程、港口万吨级码头泊位新增通过能力数据来自交通运输部；铁路运输、新建铁路投产里程、增新建铁路复线投产里程、电气化铁路投产里程数据来自中国国家铁路集团有限公司；民航运输、新增民用运输机场数据来自中国民用航空局；管道运输数据来自中国石油天然气集团有限公司、中国石油化工集团有限公司、中国海洋石油集团有限公司、国家石油天然气管网集团有限公司；民用汽车保有量、道路交通事故数据来自公安部；邮政业务数据来自国家邮政局；通信业、软件业务收入、新增光缆线路长度等数据来自工业和信息化部；互联网上网人数、互联网普及率数据来自中国互联网络信息中心；棚户区改造、保障性租赁住房数据来自住房和城乡建设部；货物进出口数据来自海关总署；服务进出口、外商直接投资、对外直接投资、对外承包工程、对外劳务合作等数据来自商务部；财政数据来自财政部；新增减税降费数据来自国家税务总局；货币金融、公司信用类债券数据来自中国人民银行；境内交易场所筹资数据来自中国证券监督管理委员会；保险业数据来自中国银行保险监督管理委员会；医疗保险、生育保险数据来自国家医疗保障局；城乡低保、农村特困人员救助供养、临时救助、民政服务数据来自民政部；优抚对象数据来自退役军人事务部；国家自然科学基金资助项目数据来自国家自然科学基金委员会；国家重点实验室、国家科技成果转化引导基金、国家级科技企业孵化器、国家备案众创空间、技术合同等数据来自科学技术部；国家工程研究中心、国家企业技术中心、大众创业万众创新示范基地等数据来自国家发展和改革委员会；专利、商标数据来自国家知识产权局；宇航发射数据来自国家国防科技工业局；教育数据来自教育部；艺术表演团体、博物馆、公共图书馆、文化馆、旅游数据来自文化和旅游部；电视、广播数据来自国家广播电视总局；电影数据来自国家电影局；报纸、期刊、图书数据来自国家新闻出版署；档案数据来自国家档案局；医疗卫生数据来自国家卫生健康委员会；体育数据来自国家体育总局；残疾人运动员数据来自中国残疾人联合会；国有建设用地供应、海洋灾害造成直接经济损失数据来自自然资源部；平均气温、台风登陆数据来自中国气象局；农作物受灾面积、洪涝和地质灾害造成直接经济损失、干旱灾害造成直接经济损失、低温冷冻和雪灾造成直接经济损失、地震次数、地震灾害造成直接经济损失、森林火灾、受害森林面积、生产安全事故数据来自应急管理部；其他数据均来自国家统计局。

STATISTICAL COMMUNIQUÉ OF THE PEOPLE'S REPUBLIC OF CHINA ON THE 2021 NATIONAL ECONOMIC AND SOCIAL DEVELOPMENT[1]

National Bureau of Statistics of China
February 28, 2022

The year 2021 is a year of milestone significance in the history of the Communist Party of China and the People's Republic of China. Under the strong leadership of the Central Committee of the Communist Party of China (CPC) with Comrade Xi Jinping as the core, all regions and departments took Xi Jinping Thought on Socialism with Chinese Characteristics for a New Era as the guideline, fully implemented the spirits of the 19th CPC National Congress and the Plenary Sessions of the 19th Central Committee of the CPC and fostered the great founding spirit of the CPC. All regions and departments followed the decisions and arrangements made by the CPC Central Committee and the State Council, committed to the general working guideline of making progress while maintaining stability, fully and faithfully implemented the new development philosophy on all fronts, accelerated fostering a new development pattern, comprehensively

1. All figures in this Communiqué are preliminary statistics. Statistics in this Communiqué do not include Hong Kong SAR, Macao SAR and Taiwan Province. Due to the rounding-off reasons, the subentries may not add up to the aggregate totals.

deepened the reform and opening up, insisted on innovation-driven development, and promoted the high-quality development. We celebrated the centenary of the founding of the CPC, fulfilled the First Centenary Goal, and embarked on the new journey to achieve the Second Centenary Goal. While responding with composure to changes and the pandemic both unseen in a century, we have made new advances in fostering a new development pattern and pursuing high-quality development, and got off to a good start in implementing the 14th Five-Year Plan. China has maintained the leading position in the economic growth and the epidemic prevention and control in the world. National strategic capacity in science and technology accelerated its growth, industrial chain resilience was improved, reform and opening-up was advanced in depth, people's livelihood was strongly and effectively safeguarded, and ecological conservation was carried forward. These are the results of the strong leadership of the Central Committee of the CPC with Comrade Xi Jinping as the core and the results of concerted efforts and hard work by the Party and the Chinese people of all ethnic groups.

I. General Outlook

According to preliminary estimation, the gross domestic product (GDP)[2] in 2021 was 114,367.0 billion yuan, up by 8.1 percent over the previous year with the average two-year growth[3] of 5.1 percent. Of this total, the value added of the primary industry was 8,308.6 billion yuan, up by 7.1 percent over the previous year, that of the secondary industry was 45,090.4 billion yuan, up by 8.2 percent and that of the tertiary industry was 60,968.0 billion yuan, up by 8.2 percent. The value added of the primary industry accounted for 7.3 percent of the GDP; that of the secondary industry accounted for 39.4 percent; and that of the tertiary industry accounted for 53.3 percent. The contribution of the final consumption expenditure to GDP growth rate was up by 5.3 percentage points, that of the gross capital formation to GDP growth rate up by 1.1 percentage points and that of the net exports of goods and services to GDP growth rate up by 1.7 percentage points. The per capita GDP in 2021 was 80,976 yuan, up by 8.0 percent over the previous year. The gross national income[4] in 2021 was 113,351.8 billion yuan, up by 7.9 percent over the previous year. The overall labor productivity[5] was 146,380 yuan per person in 2021, up by 8.7 percent over the previous year.

---

2. Gross domestic product (GDP), value added of the three and related industries, regional GDP, per capita GDP and gross national income (GNI) as quoted in this Communiqué are calculated at current prices whereas their growth rates are at constant prices.

3. The average two-year growth is the geometric mean of the growth with the data of the same period in 2019 as the base.

4. Gross national income, also known as gross national product, refers to the total primary distribution of the income created by all the resident units of a country (or a region) during a certain period of time. It equals to gross domestic product plus the net primary distribution of income from abroad.

5. The overall labor productivity refers to the ratio between the GDP (at 2020 constant prices) and the total number of persons employed. Historical data were revised according to the results of the Seventh National Population Census.

Figure 1: Gross Domestic Product and Growth Rates 2017-2021

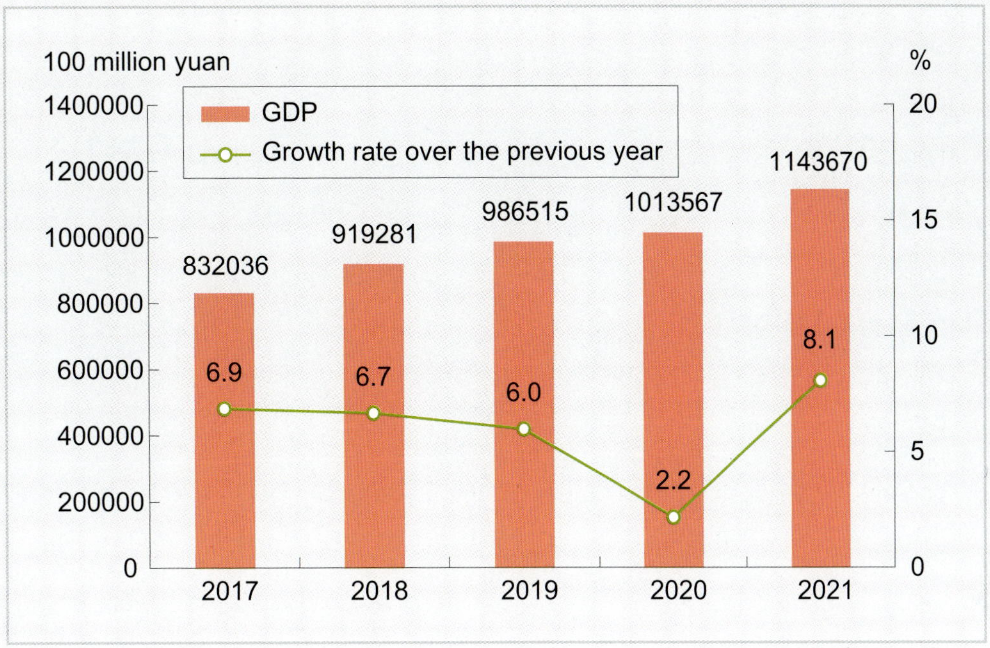

Figure 2: Shares of the Three Industries' Value Added of GDP 2017-2021

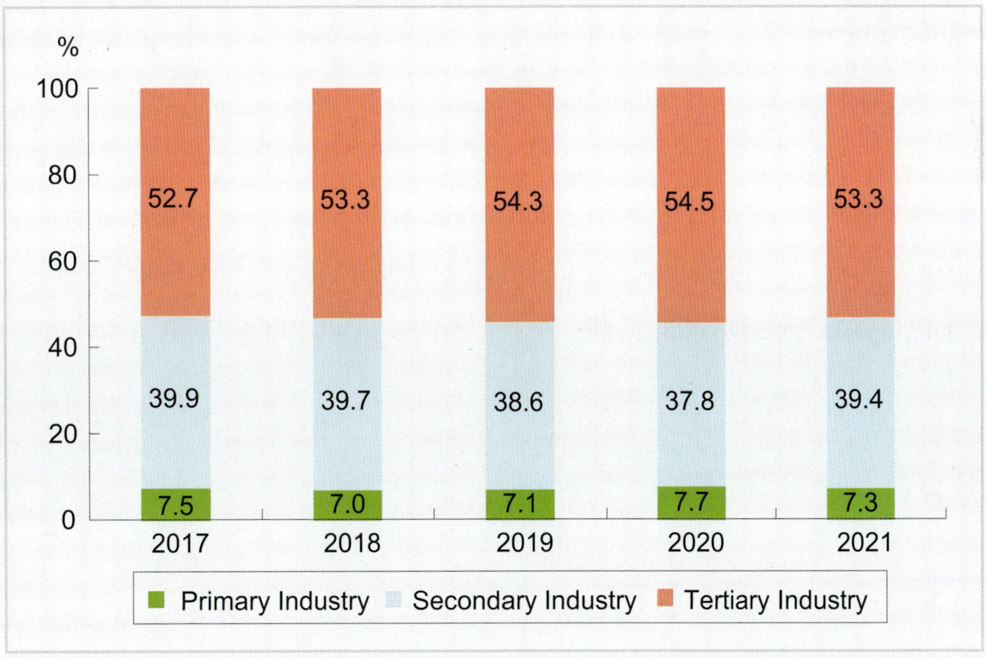

Figure 3: The Overall Labor Productivity 2017-2021[6]

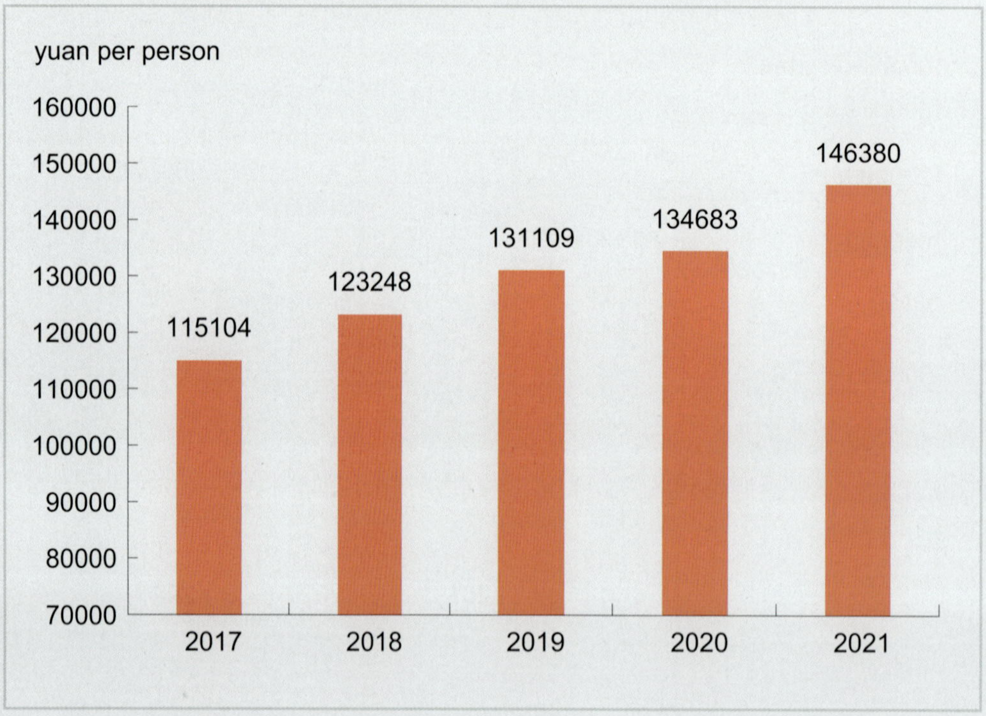

By the end of 2021, the total number of national population[7] reached 1,412.60 million, an increase of 0.48 million over that at the end of 2020. Of this total, urban permanent residents numbered 914.25 million. There were 10.62 million births in 2021 with a crude birth rate of 7.52 per thousand; and there were 10.14 million deaths with a crude death rate of 7.18 per thousand. The natural growth rate was 0.34 per thousand. The number of population who live in places other than their household registration areas[8] reached 504 million, of which 385 million were floating population[9].

6. See note 5.

7. The national population refers to the population of the 31 provinces, autonomous regions and municipalities directly under the central government and servicemen of the Chinese mainland, excluding residents of Hong Kong, Macao and Taiwan and foreigners living in the 31 provinces, autonomous regions and municipalities directly under the central government.

8. Population who live in places other than their household registration areas refers to those who reside in areas other than their household registration and have been away from there for over 6 months.

9. Floating population refers to population who live in places other than their household registration excluding those with current residences different from the places of their household registration but still in the same city. Population who live in places other than their household registration but still in the same city refers to those whose current residences are different from the registered towns or streets in the same district or in different districts but still in the same municipality or prefecture-level city.

Table 1: Population and Its Composition by the End of 2021

Item	Population at Year-end (10,000 persons)	Proportion (%)
National Total	**141260**	**100.0**
Of which: Urban	91425	64.7
Rural	49835	35.3
Of which: Male	72311	51.2
Female	68949	48.8
Of which: Aged 0-15 (under the age of 16)[10]	26302	18.6
Aged 16-59 (under the age of 60)	88222	62.5
Aged 60 and above	26736	18.9
Of which: Aged 65 and above	20056	14.2

At the end of 2021, the number of employed people in China was 746.52 million, and that in urban areas was 467.73 million, accounting for 62.7 percent for the total employed people, 1.1 percentage points higher than that at the end of the previous year. The newly increased employed people in urban areas numbered 12.69 million in 2021, 0.83 million more than the previous year. The surveyed urban unemployment rate in 2021 averaged 5.1 percent. The surveyed urban unemployment rate at the year end was 5.1 percent, and the registered urban unemployment rate was 3.96 percent. The total number of migrant workers[11] was 292.51 million, up by 2.4 percent over that of 2020. Specifically, the number of migrant workers who left their hometowns and worked in other places was 171.72 million, up by 1.3 percent, and those who worked in their own localities reached 120.79 million, up by 4.1 percent.

Figure 4: Newly Increased Employed People in Urban Areas 2017-2021

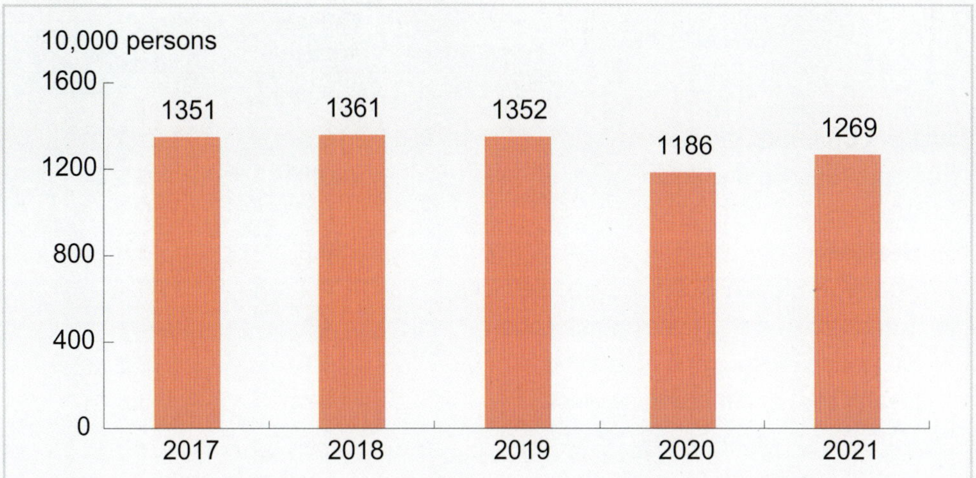

10. By the end of 2021, the population aged 0 to 14 (under the age of 15) was 246.78 million and that aged 15 to 59 (under the age of 60) was 898.46 million.

11. The number of migrant workers includes those who are employed outside their villages and towns for more than six months in the year and those who are engaged in non-agricultural work in their villages and towns for more than six months in the year.

The consumer prices in 2021 went up by 0.9 percent over the previous year. The producer prices for industrial products went up by 8.1 percent and the purchasing prices for industrial producers up by 11.0 percent. The producer prices for farm products[12] dropped by 2.2 percent. In December, out of the 70 large and medium-sized cities, 53 cities experienced a year-on-year rise in sales prices of new commercial residential buildings and 17 cities experienced a decline; 43 cities experienced a year-on-year rise in sales prices of second-hand housing, one city maintained the same, and 26 cities experienced a decline.

Figure 5: Monthly Changes of Consumer Prices in 2021

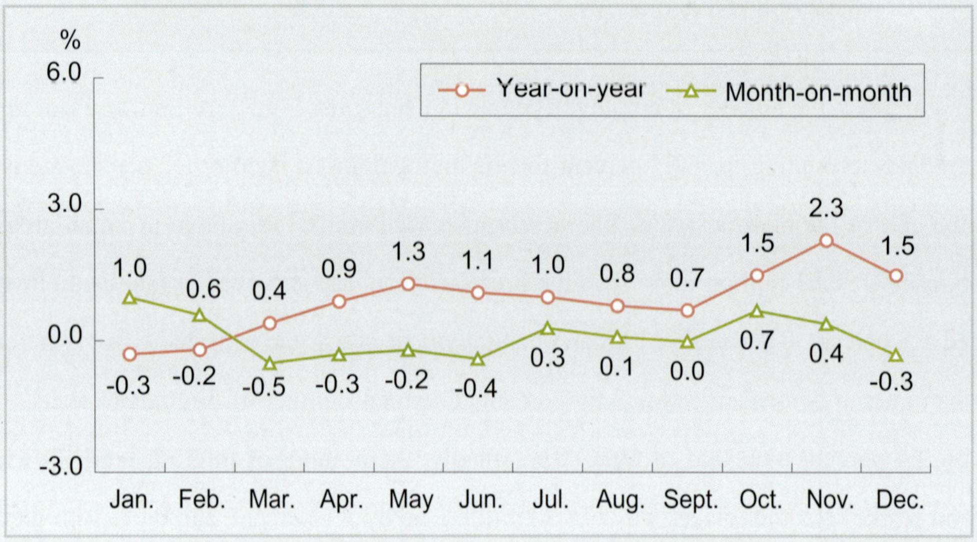

Table 2: Changes of Consumer Prices in 2021

Unit: %

Item	National Average	Urban	Rural
General level of consumer prices	**0.9**	**1.0**	**0.7**
Of which: Food, tobacco and liquor	-0.3	0.0	-1.2
Clothing	0.3	0.3	0.0
Residence[13]	0.8	0.8	1.1
Household facilities, articles and services	0.4	0.4	0.4
Transportation and telecommunication	4.1	4.2	3.9
Education, culture and recreation	1.9	2.0	1.7
Health care and medical services	0.4	0.3	0.7
Miscellaneous goods and services	-1.3	-1.4	-1.2

12. The producer prices for farm products refer to the prices of farm products sold directly by producers.
13. The prices for residence include prices for rent, maintenance and management, water, electricity and fuel etc.

At the end of 2021, China's foreign exchange reserves reached 3,250.2 billion US dollars, an increase of 33.6 billion US dollars compared with that at the end of 2020. The average exchange rate of the year was 6.4515 RMB to 1 USD dollar, appreciated by 6.9 percent over that of 2020.

Figure 6: Year-end China's Foreign Exchange Reserves 2017-2021

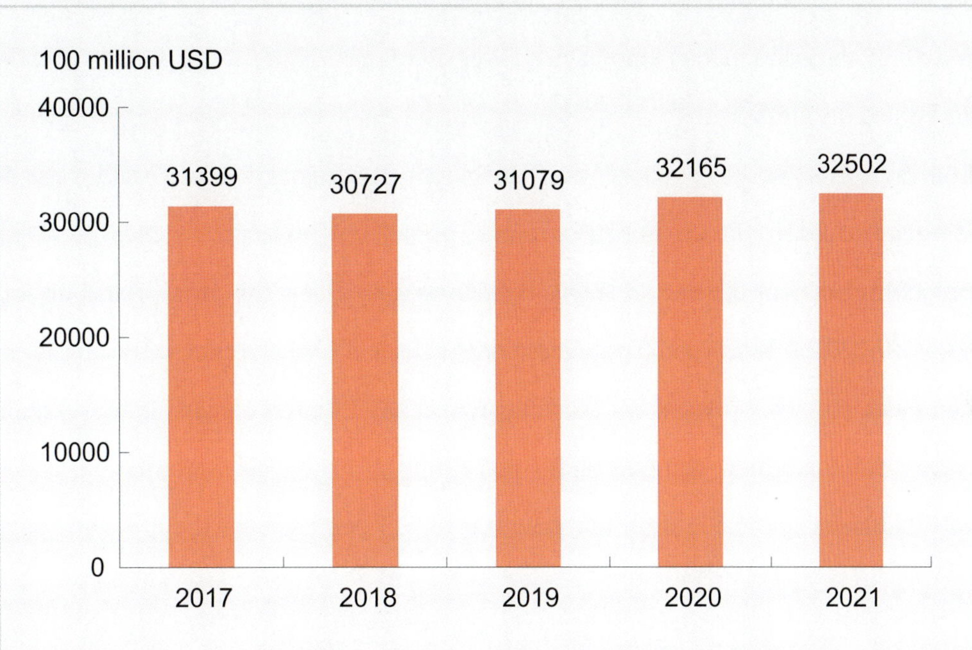

New industries, new forms and models of business gathered speed to grow. Among the industries above the designated size, the value added of the high technology manufacturing industry[14] increased by 18.2 percent over the previous year, accounting for 15.1 percent of that of all industrial enterprises above the designated size. The value added for the manufacture of equipment[15] was up by 12.9 percent, accounting for 32.4 percent of that of all industrial enterprises above the designated size. Among the service enterprises above the designated size[16], the business revenue of the strategic emerging service industries[17] went up

14. High technology manufacturing industry includes manufacture of medicine, manufacture of aerospace vehicle and equipment, manufacture of electronic and communication equipment, manufacture of computers and office equipment, manufacture of medical equipment, manufacture of measuring instrument and equipment and manufacture of optical and photographic equipment.

15. Manufacture of equipment includes manufacture of metal products, general purpose equipment, special purpose equipment, automobiles, railway, ship, aerospace and other transport equipment, electrical machinery and apparatus, computers, communication and other electric equipment and measuring instrument and machinery.

16. Service enterprises above the designated size refer to legal entities of transport, storage and post, information transmission, software and information technology services, water conservancy, environment and public facilities management, and health with annual business revenue of 20 million yuan and above; legal entities of real estate (excluding real estate development and operation), leasing and business services, scientific research and technology services and education with annual business revenue of 10 million yuan and above; and legal entities of services to households, repair and other services and culture, sports and entertainment, and social services with annual business revenue of 5 million and above.

17. Strategic emerging service industries refer to the related service sectors of information technology of new generation, manufacture of high-end equipment, new materials, biotech, new energy vehicles, new energy, energy-saving and environmental protection and digital creative industries, and service industries related to new technology, innovation and entrepreneurship. The growth rate of the business revenue of the strategic emerging service industries in 2021 was calculated on a comparable basis.

by 16.0 percent compared with the previous year. In 2021, the investment in high technology industries[18] increased by 17.1 percent over the previous year. In 2021, the output of new energy vehicles reached 3.677 million, up by 152.5 percent compared with the previous year; and that of integrated circuits was 359.43 billion, up by 37.5 percent. In 2021, the online retail sales[19] reached 13,088.4 billion yuan, up by 14.1 percent over the previous year on comparable basis. In 2021, the number of newly registered market entities was 28.87 million with 25 thousand market entities newly registered per day on average. By the end of 2021, the market entities totaled 0.15 billion.

Solid progress was made in the coordinated development across urban and rural areas and different regions. By the end of 2021, the urbanization rate of permanent residents reached 64.72 percent, 0.83 percentage points higher than the end of 2020. By region[20], in 2021, the gross domestic product in the eastern areas was 59,220.2 billion yuan, an increase of 8.1 percent over the previous year; the central areas, 25,013.2 billion yuan, up by 8.7 percent; the western areas, 23,971.0 billion yuan, up by 7.4 percent; and the northeastern areas, 5,569.9 billion yuan, up by 6.1 percent. In 2021, the gross domestic product in Beijing-Tianjin-Hebei Region reached 9,635.6 billion yuan, up by 7.3 percent over the previous year; that in the Yangtze River Economic Belt, 53,022.8 billion yuan, up by 8.7 percent; and that in the Yangtze River Delta, 27,605.4 billion yuan, up by 8.4 percent. Major regional strategies such as the construction of Guangdong-Hong Kong-Macao Greater Bay Areas, the ecological protection of the Yellow River Basin, and the high-quality development were further implemented.

---

18. Investment in high technology industries refers to investment in six high technology manufacturing industries, including the manufacture of medicine and manufacture of aerospace vehicle and equipment, and nine high technology service industries, including information service and e-commerce service.

19. Online retail sales refer to the retail sales of goods and services realized through internet trading platforms (online platforms mainly in trading physical commodities, including self-built websites and third-party platforms).

20.The eastern areas include 10 provinces and municipalities: Beijing, Tianjin, Hebei, Shanghai, Jiangsu, Zhejiang, Fujian, Shandong, Guangdong and Hainan; the central areas cover 6 provinces: Shanxi, Anhui, Jiangxi, Henan, Hubei and Hunan; the western areas include 12 provinces, autonomous regions and municipalities: Inner Mongolia, Guangxi, Chongqing, Sichuan, Guizhou, Yunnan, Tibet, Shaanxi, Gansu, Qinghai, Ningxia and Xinjiang; the northeastern areas include 3 provinces: Liaoning, Jilin and Heilongjiang.

Figure 7: Year-end Urbanization Rates of Permanent Residents 2017-2021[21]

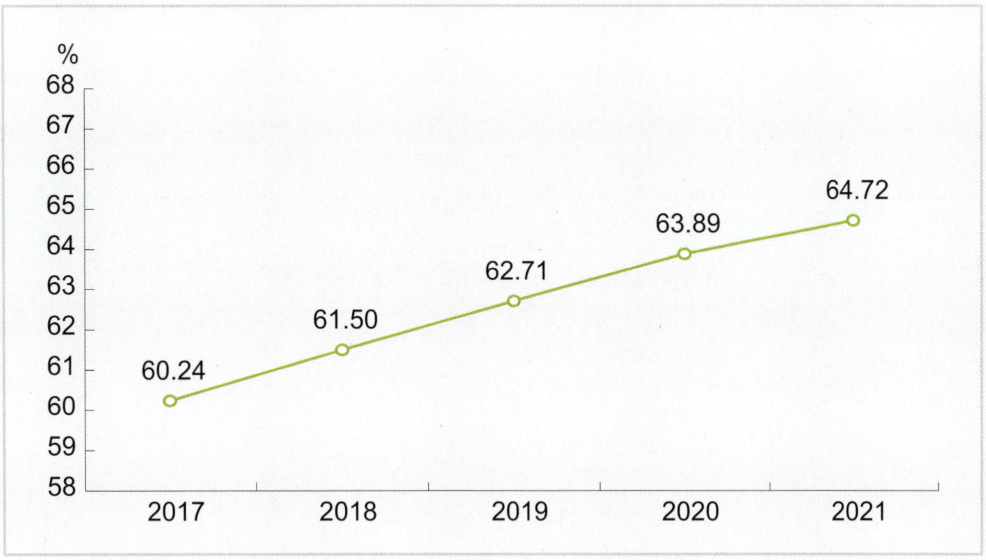

New achievement was made in ecological environmental protection. The national energy consumption per 10,000 yuan worth of GDP[22] in 2021 dropped by 2.7 percent over the previous year. Of the monitored 339 cities at prefecture level and above, 64.3 percent reached the air quality standard and 35.7 percent failed. The annual average concentration of particulate matter ($PM_{2.5}$) was 30 micrograms per cubic meter, down by 9.1 percent over the previous year. Of the 3,641 sections under the national monitoring program for surface water, 84.9 percent were fairly clean water quality (Grade I to III), 11.8 percent were Grade IV, 2.2 percent were Grade V and 1.2 percent was worse than Grade V national standard.

II. Agriculture

In 2021, the sown area of grain was 117.63 million hectares, an increase of 0.86 million hectares compared with that in 2020. Of this total, the sown area of rice was 29.92 million hectares, a decrease of 0.15 million hectares; the sown area of wheat was 23.57 million hectares, an increase of 0.19 million hectares; the sown area of corn was 43.32 million hectares, an increase of 2.06 million hectares. The sown area of cotton was 3.03 million hectares, a decrease of 0.14 million hectares. The sown area of oil-bearing crops was 13.10 million hectares, a decrease of 30 thousand hectares; the sown area of sugar crops was 1.46 million hectares, a decrease of 0.11 million hectares.

The total output of grain in 2021 was 682.85 million tons, an increase of 13.36 million tons over the

21.The year-end urbanization rates of permanent residents from 2017 to 2019 were revised according to the results of the Seventh National Population Census.

22.The energy consumption per 10,000 yuan worth of GDP is calculated at 2020 constant prices.

previous year, or up by 2.0 percent. Of this total, the output of summer crops was 145.96 million tons, up by 2.2 percent, and that of the early rice was 28.02 million tons, up by 2.7 percent. The output of autumn grain was 508.88 million tons, up by 1.9 percent. The output of cereal in 2021 was 632.76 million tons, up by 2.6 percent over 2020, among which the output of rice was 212.84 million tons, up by 0.5 percent; that of wheat was 136.95 million tons, up by 2.0 percent; and that of corn was 272.55 million tons, up by 4.6 percent.

Figure 8: Output of Grain 2017-2021

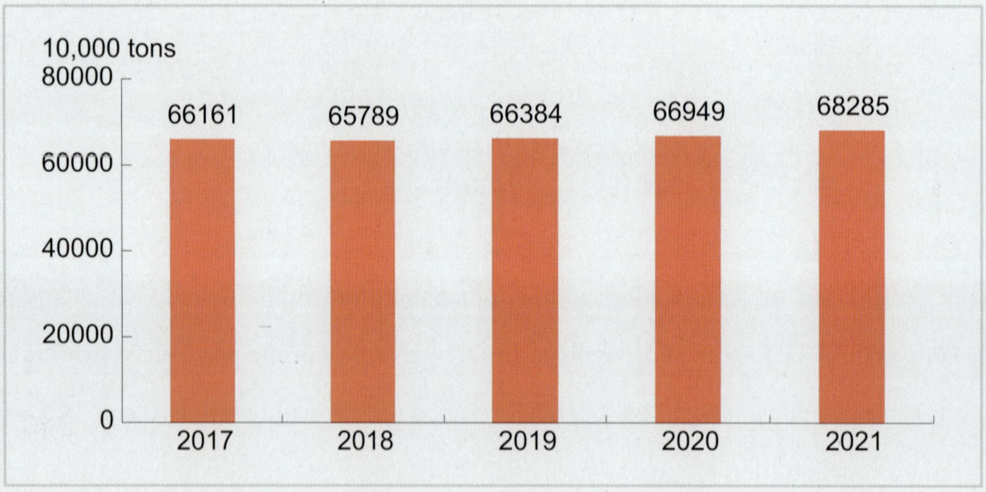

In 2021, the output of cotton was 5.73 million tons, down by 3.0 percent over the previous year, that of oil-bearing crops was 36.13 million tons, up by 0.8 percent, that of sugar crops was 114.51 million tons, down by 4.7 percent, and that of tea was 3.18 million tons, up by 8.3 percent.

The total output of pork, beef, mutton and poultry in 2021 was 88.87 million tons, up by 16.3 percent over the previous year. Of this total, the output of pork was 52.96 million tons, up by 28.8 percent; that of beef was 6.98 million tons, up by 3.7 percent; that of mutton was 5.14 million tons, up by 4.4 percent; and that of poultry was 23.80 million tons, up by 0.8 percent. The total output of eggs was 34.09 million tons, down by 1.7 percent. The output of milk was 36.83 million tons, up by 7.1 percent. At the end of the year, 449.22 million pigs were registered in the total stocks, up by 10.5 percent compared with that at the end of 2020, and 671.28 million pigs were slaughtered, up by 27.4 percent over the previous year.

The total output of aquatic products in 2021 was 66.93 million tons, up by 2.2 percent over the previous year. Of this total, the output of cultured aquatic products was 53.88 million tons, up by 3.1 percent; and that of fished aquatic products was 13.05 million tons, down by 1.5 percent.

The total production of timber in 2021 reached 98.88 million cubic meters, down by 3.6 percent over the previous year.

In 2021, over 0.46 million hectares of farmland were newly equipped with irrigation systems and another 1.88 million hectares of farmland was newly equipped with water-saving irrigation systems.

III. Industry and Construction

In 2021, the total value added of the industrial sector was 37,257.5 billion yuan, up by 9.6 percent over the previous year. The value added of industrial enterprises above the designated size increased by 9.6 percent. Of the industrial enterprises above the designated size, in terms of ownership, the value added of the state-holding enterprises was up by 8.0 percent, that of the share-holding enterprises up by 9.8 percent, that of the enterprises funded by foreign investors and investors from Hong Kong, Macao and Taiwan up by 8.9 percent and that of private enterprises up by 10.2 percent. In terms of sectors, the value added of the mining industry was up by 5.3 percent, that of manufacturing up by 9.8 percent and that of production and supply of electricity, heat power, gas and water up by 11.4 percent.

Figure 9: Value Added and Growth Rates of Industrial Enterprises 2017-2021

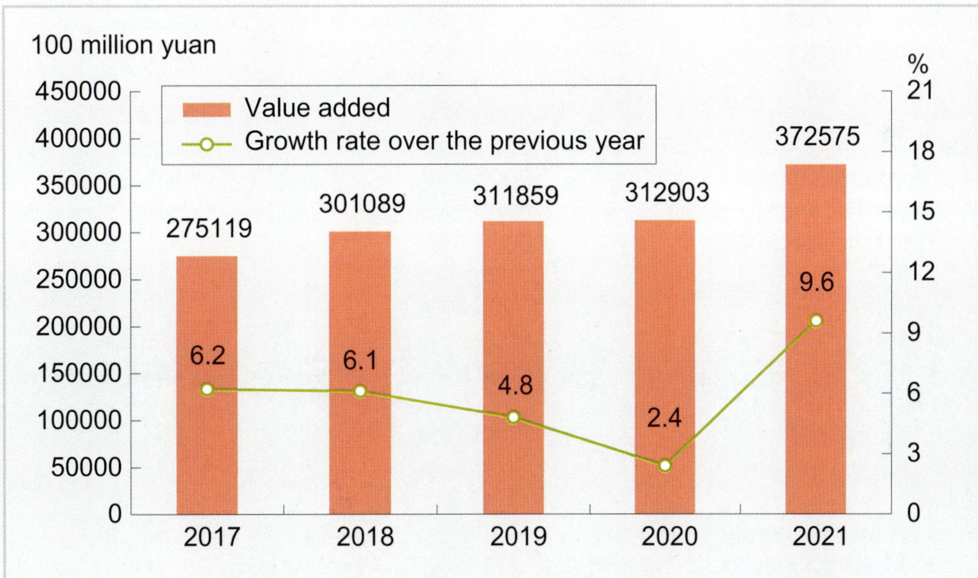

In 2021, of the industrial enterprises above the designated size, the value added for processing of food from agricultural and sideline products was up by 7.7 percent over the previous year; for textile industry up by 1.4 percent; for manufacture of raw chemical materials and chemical products up by 7.7 percent; for manufacture of non-metallic mineral products up by 8.0 percent; for smelting and pressing of ferrous metals up by 1.2 percent; for manufacture of general purpose machinery up by 12.4 percent; for manufacture of special purpose machinery up by 12.6 percent; for manufacture of automobiles up by 5.5 percent; for manufacture of electrical machinery and apparatus up by 16.8 percent; for manufacture of computers, communication equipment and other electronic equipment up by 15.7 percent; for production and supply of electricity and heat power up by 10.9 percent.

Table 3: Output of Major Industrial Products and Growth Rates in 2021[23]

Product	Unit	Output	Increase over 2020 (%)
Yarn	10000 tons	2873.7	9.8
Cloth	100 million meters	502.0	9.3
Chemical fiber	10000 tons	6708.5	9.5
Refined sugar (final product)	10000 tons	1482.3	3.6
Cigarettes	100 million	24182.4	1.3
Color TV sets	10000	18496.5	-5.8
Of which: LCD TV sets	10000	17424.3	-9.5
Household refrigerators	10000	8992.1	-0.3
Air conditioners	10000	21835.7	3.8
Primary energy output	100 million tons of standard coal equivalent	43.3	6.2
Coal	100 million tons	41.3	5.7
Crude petroleum oil	10000 tons	19888.1	2.1
Natural gas	100 million cubic meters	2075.8	7.8
Electricity	100 million kilowatt-hours	85342.5	9.7
Of which: Thermal power[24]	100 million kilowatt-hours	58058.7	8.9
Hydropower	100 million kilowatt-hours	13390.0	-1.2
Nuclear-power	100 million kilowatt-hours	4075.2	11.3
Crude steel	10000 tons	103524.3	-2.8
Rolled steel[25]	10000 tons	133666.8	0.9
Ten kinds of nonferrous metals	10000 tons	6477.1	4.7
Of which: Refined copper (copper)	10000 tons	1048.7	4.6
Aluminum electrolyze	10000 tons	3850.3	3.8
Cement	100 million tons	23.8	-0.4
Sulfuric acid (100%)	10000 tons	9382.7	1.6
Caustic soda (100%)	10000 tons	3891.3	5.9
Ethylene	10000 tons	2825.7	30.8
Chemical fertilizers (100 percent equivalent)	10000 tons	5543.6	0.9
Power generation equipment	10000 kilowatts	15954.6	19.2
Motor vehicles	10000	2652.8	4.8
Of which: Basic passenger cars (cars)	10000	976.5	5.7
Sport utility vehicles (SUVs)	10000	973.6	7.6
Large and medium tractors	10000	41.2	19.4
Integrated circuits	100 million pieces	3594.3	37.5
Program-controlled switchboards	10000 lines	699.6	-0.4
Mobile telephones	10000	166151.6	13.1
Micro computer equipment	10000	46692.0	23.5
Industrial robots	10000 sets	36.6	67.9

23. Output data of some products were verified and adjusted in 2020; the growth rates of output in 2021 were calculated on a comparable basis.

24. Thermal power refers to electricity generated by coal, oil, gas, residual heat, pressure and gas, waste incineration and biomass.

25. The data included the steel reprocessed among enterprises.

By the end of 2021, the installed power generation capacity was 2,376.92 million kilowatts, up by 7.9 percent over that at the end of 2020, among which[26] the installed thermal power generation capacity was 1,296.78 million kilowatts, up by 4.1 percent; the installed hydropower generation capacity was 390.92 million kilowatts, up by 5.6 percent; the installed nuclear power generation capacity was 53.26 million kilowatts, up by 6.8 percent. The installed grid-connected wind power generation capacity was 328.48 million kilowatts, up by 16.6 percent and the installed grid-connected solar power generation capacity was 306.56 million kilowatts, up by 20.9 percent.

In 2021, the profits made by industrial enterprises above the designated size were 8,709.2 billion yuan, up by 34.3 percent over the previous year[27]. By ownership, the profits of state-holding enterprises were 2,277.0 billion yuan, up by 56.0 percent over the previous year; those of share-holding enterprises were 6,270.2 billion yuan, up by 40.2 percent; those of enterprises funded by foreign investors or investors from Hong Kong, Macao and Taiwan were 2,284.6 billion yuan, up by 21.1 percent; and those of private enterprises were 2,915.0 billion yuan, up by 27.6 percent. In terms of different sectors, the profits of mining were 1,039.1 billion yuan, up by 190.7 percent over the previous year; those of manufacturing were 7,361.2 billion yuan, up by 31.6 percent; and those of the production and supply of electricity, heat power, gas and water were 308.9 billion yuan, down by 41.9 percent. In 2021, the cost for per-hundred-yuan business revenue of the industrial enterprises above the designated size was 83.74 yuan, or 0.23 yuan less than that of 2020; the profit rate of the business revenue was 6.81 percent, up by 0.76 percentage points. By the end of 2021, the asset-liability ratio of industrial enterprises above the designated size was 56.1 percent, 0.1 percentage points lower than the end of 2020. The national industrial capacity utilization rate[28] was 77.5 percent in 2021.

In 2021, the value added of construction enterprises in China was 8,013.8 billion yuan, up by 2.1 percent over the previous year. The profits made by construction enterprises qualified for general contracts and specialized contracts reached 855.4 billion yuan, up by 1.3 percent over the previous year, of which the profits made by state-holding enterprises were 362.0 billion yuan, up by 8.0 percent.

26. A few installed power generation capacity (e.g. geothermal) is not listed.

27. The growth rates and rate changes of financial indicators of industrial enterprises above the designated size in 2021 were calculated on a comparable basis due to adjustments of data coverage in the statistical programmes, statistical law enforcement and removal of duplicated data.

28. Capacity utilization rate refers to the ratio of the actual production to the production capacity (in terms of value). Actual production refers to the total industrial output value during the enterprise's reporting period. Production capacity refers to the production which can be realized and sustained for a long term under the condition of the supply of labor force, materials, fuel and transportation guaranteed and the production equipment in proper operation.

Figure 10: Value Added and Growth Rates of Construction Industry 2017-2021

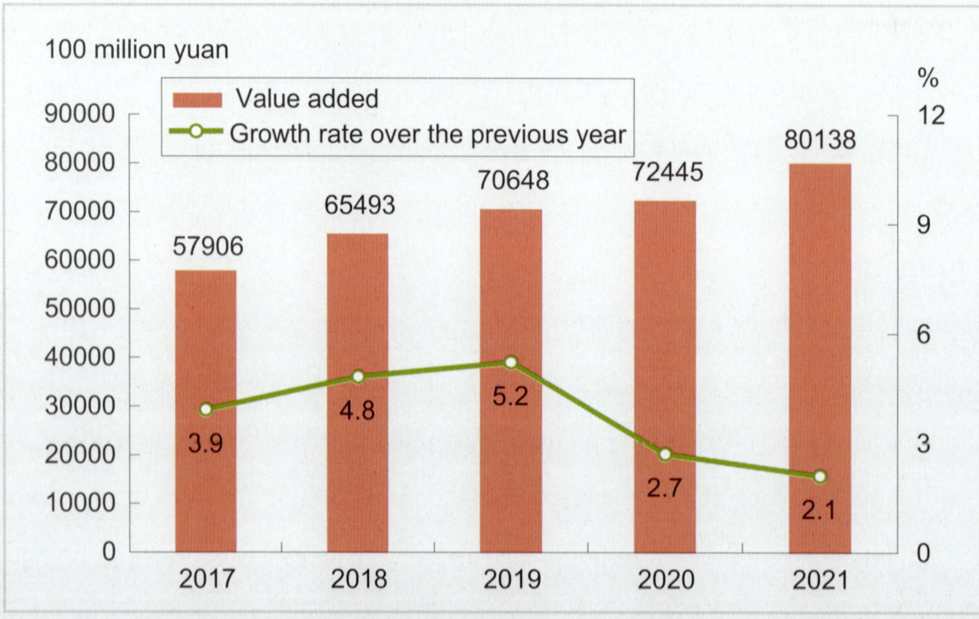

IV. Service Sector

In 2021, the value added of the wholesale and retail trades was 11,049.3 billion yuan, up by 11.3 percent over the previous year; that of transport, storage and post was 4,706.1 billion yuan, up by 12.1 percent; that of hotels and catering services was 1,785.3 billion yuan, up by 14.5 percent; that of financial intermediation was 9,120.6 billion yuan, up by 4.8 percent; that of real estate was 7,756.1 billion yuan, up by 5.2 percent; that of information transmission, software and information technology services was 4,395.6 billion yuan, up by 17.2 percent; and that of leasing and business services was 3,535.0 billion yuan, up by 6.2 percent. In 2021, the business revenue of service enterprises above the designated size grew by 18.7 percent over the previous year, and the operating profits increased by 13.4 percent.

Figure 11: Value Added and Growth Rates of Service Sector 2017-2021

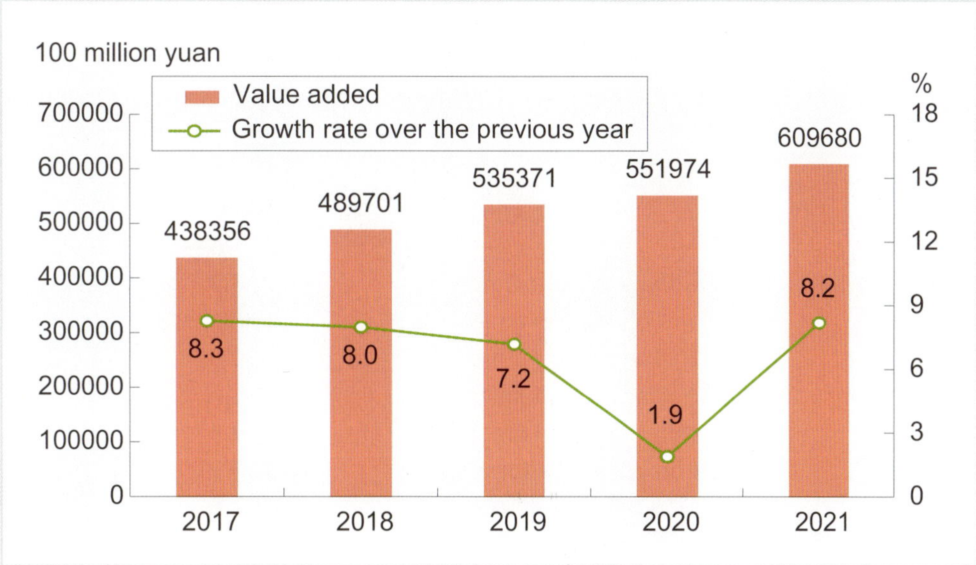

The total freight traffic[29] in 2021 reached 53.0 billion tons. The freight flows were 22,357.4 billion ton-kilometers. The volume of freight handled by ports throughout the year totaled 15.5 billion tons, up by 6.8 percent over the previous year, of which the freight for foreign trade was 4.7 billion tons, up by 4.5 percent. Container shipping of ports reached 282.72 million standard containers, up by 7.0 percent.

Table 4: Freight Traffic by All Means of Transportation and Growth Rates in 2021

Item	Unit	Volume	Increase over 2020(%)
Total freight traffic	**100 million tons**	**529.7**	**12.3**
Railways	100 million tons	47.2	5.9
Highways	100 million tons	391.4	14.2
Waterways	100 million tons	82.4	8.2
Civil aviation	10000 tons	731.8	8.2
Pipelines	100 million tons	8.7	5.7
Freight flows	**100 million ton-kilometers**	**223574.4**	**13.7**
Railways	100 million ton-kilometers	33190.7	9.3
Highways	100 million ton-kilometers	69087.7	14.8
Waterways	100 million ton-kilometers	115577.5	9.2
Civil aviation	100 million ton-kilometers	278.2	15.8
Pipelines	100 million ton-kilometers	5440.3	4.9

29. The total freight traffic and flows include the traffic and flows by railways, highways, waterways, civil aviation and pipelines and the growth rates in 2021 were calculated on a comparable basis.

In 2021, the total passenger traffic was 8.3 billion person-times, down by 14.1 percent over 2020, and the passenger flows were 1,975.8 billion person-kilometers, up by 2.6 percent.

Table 5: Passenger Traffic by All Means of Transportation and Growth Rates in 2021

Item	Unit	Volume	Increase over 2020(%)
Total passenger traffic	**100 million person-times**	**83.0**	**-14.1**
Railways	100 million person-times	26.1	18.5
Highways	100 million person-times	50.9	-26.2
Waterways	100 million person-times	1.6	9.0
Civil aviation	100 million person-times	4.4	5.5
Passenger flows	**100 million person-kilometers**	**19758.2**	**2.6**
Railways	100 million person-kilometers	9567.8	15.7
Highways	100 million person-kilometers	3627.5	-21.8
Waterways	100 million person-kilometers	33.1	0.4
Civil aviation	100 million person-kilometers	6529.7	3.5

The total number of motor vehicles for civilian use reached 301.51 million (including 7.32 million tri-wheel motor vehicles and low-speed trucks) by the end of 2021, up by 20.64 million over that at the end of 2020, of which the privately-owned vehicles numbered 262.46 million, an increase of 18.52 million. The total number of cars for civilian use was 167.39 million, an increase of 10.99 million, of which the privately-owned cars numbered 157.32 million, an increase of 10.59 million.

The turnover of post services[30] totaled 1,369.8 billion yuan, up by 25.1 percent over the previous year. In 2021, the number of mail delivery was 1.09 billion; that of parcel delivery was 20 million; and that of express delivery was 108.30 billion with a revenue reaching 1,033.2 billion yuan. The turnover of telecommunication services[31] totaled 1,696.0 billion yuan, up by 27.8 percent over the previous year. By the end of 2021, there were 9.96 million mobile phone base stations[32], among which the number of 4G base stations reached 5.90 million and that of 5G base stations 1.43 million. In 2021, there were 1,823.53 million phone subscribers in China, of whom 1,642.83 million were mobile phone subscribers. The mobile phone coverage was 116.3 sets

30. The turnover of post services was calculated at the constant prices of 2020.
31. The turnover of telecommunication services was calculated at the constant prices of 2020.
32. The number of mobile phone base stations refers to the total number of wireless transceivers serving communities that handle the wireless communication between the base stations and mobile stations, relay between the mobile switchboards and mobile stations, and monitor the quality of wireless transmission at the end of the reporting period.

per 100 persons. The number of fixed broadband internet users[33] reached 535.79 million, an increase of 52.24 million over the end of the previous year. Of this total, fixed fiber-optic broadband internet users[34] amounted to 505.51 million, an increase of 51.36 million. Users of cellular internet of things terminals[35] totaled 1.399 billion, an increase of 0.264 billion.The number of internet user was 1.032 billion, 1.029 billion of which were mobile internet surfers[36]. The coverage of internet was 73.0 percent, and 57.6 percent in rural areas. The mobile internet traffic in 2021 was 221.6 billion gigabytes, up by 33.9 percent over the previous year. Software revenue of software and information technology services industry[37] in 2021 was 9,499.4 billion yuan, up by 17.7 percent over 2020 on a comparable basis.

Figure 12: Express Delivery and Growth Rates 2017-2021

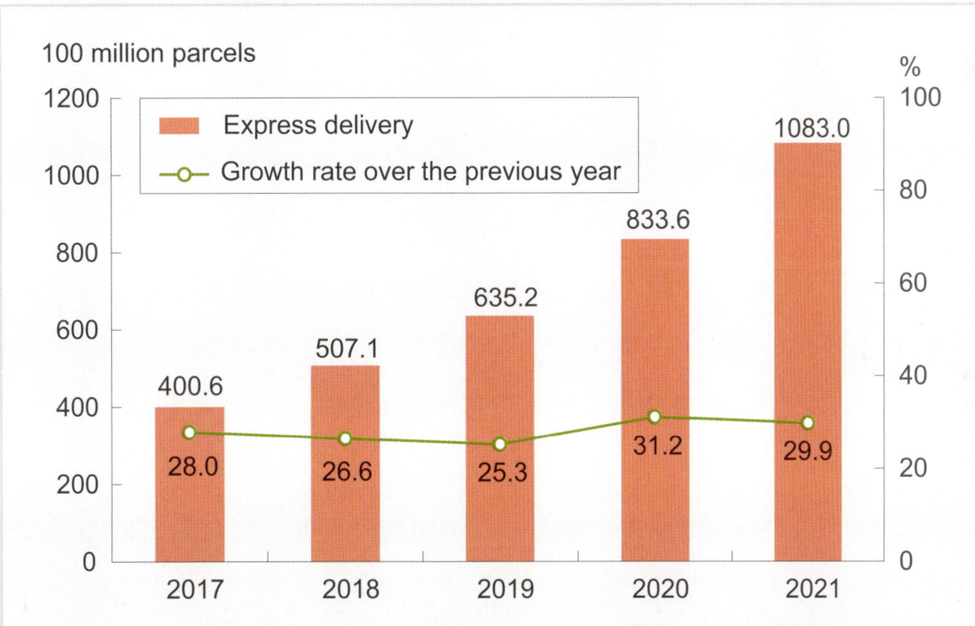

33. Fixed broadband internet users refer to those who subscribed to the telecommunication enterprises and access the Internet through xDSL, FTTx+LAN, FTTH/0 and other broadband access ways as well as general dedicated lines at the end of the reporting period.

34. Fixed fiber-optic broadband internet users refer to those who subscribed to the telecommunication enterprises and access the Internet through FTTH or FTT0 at the end of the reporting period.

35. Users of cellular internet of things terminals refer to those who access the mobile internet and subscribe to the internet of things services at the end of the reporting period. Internet of things terminals refers to the internet of things devices that connect the sensing network layer and the transmission network layer to implement remote data collection and data transmission to the network layer.

36. The number of mobile internet surfers refers to the number of people who have accessed the internet through mobile phones over the past half year.

37. Software and information technology services industry includes software development, integrated circuit design, information system integration and internet of things technology services, operation maintenance services, information processing and storage support services, IT consulting services, digital content services and other IT services industry.

Figure 13: Year-end Number of Fixed Broadband Internet Users 2017-2021

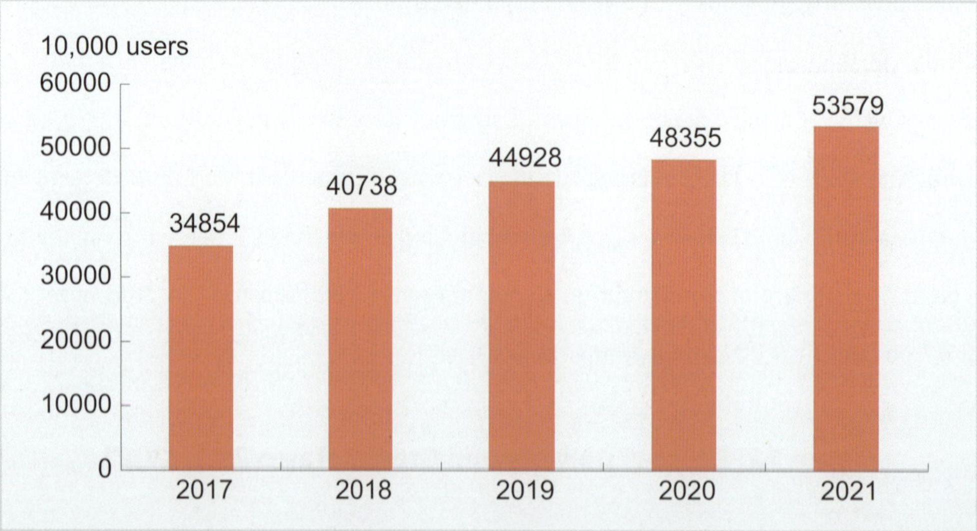

V. Domestic Trade

In 2021, the total retail sales of consumer goods reached 44,082.3 billion yuan, an increase of 12.5 percent over the previous year. An analysis on different areas showed that the retail sales of consumer goods in urban areas stood at 38,155.8 billion yuan, up by 12.5 percent, and that in rural areas reached 5,926.5 billion yuan, up by 12.1 percent. Grouped by consumption patterns, the retail sales of commodities was 39,392.8 billion yuan, up by 11.8 percent, and that of catering industry was 4,689.5 billion yuan, up by 18.6 percent.

Figure 14: Total Retail Sales of Consumer Goods and Growth Rates 2017-2021

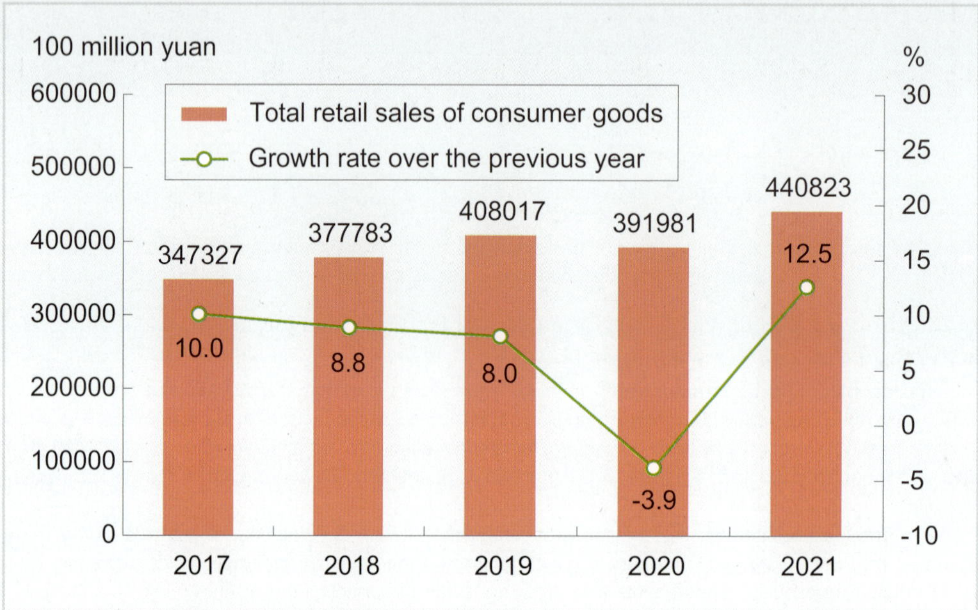

Of the total retail sales of commodities by enterprises above the designated size, the retail sales for grain, oil and food went up by 10.8 percent over the previous year; beverage up by 20.4 percent; tobacco and liquor up by 21.2 percent; clothes, shoes, hats and textiles up by 12.7 percent; cosmetics up by 14.0 percent; gold, silver and jewelry up by 29.8 percent; daily necessities up by 14.4 percent; household appliances and audio-video equipment up by 10.0 percent; traditional Chinese and western medicines up by 9.9 percent; cultural and office appliances up by 18.8 percent; furniture up by 14.5 percent; telecommunication equipment up by 14.6 percent; building and decoration materials up by 20.4 percent; petroleum and petroleum products up by 21.2 percent; and motor vehicles up by 7.6 percent.

In 2021, the online retail sales of physical goods were 10,804.2 billion yuan, up by 12.0 percent over the previous year on a comparable basis, accounting for 24.5 percent of the total retail sales of consumer goods.

VI. Investment in Fixed Assets

The total investment in fixed assets[38] of the country in 2021 was 55,288.4 billion yuan, up by 4.9 percent over the previous year. Of the total, the investment in fixed assets (excluding rural households) was 54,454.7 billion yuan, up by 4.9 percent. Of the investment in fixed assets (excluding rural households), by regions[39], the investment in eastern areas was up by 6.4 percent, central areas up by 10.2 percent, western areas up by 3.9 percent, and northeastern areas up by 5.7 percent.

Of the investment in fixed assets (excluding rural households), the investment in the primary industry was 1,427.5 billion yuan, up by 9.1 percent over the previous year; that in the secondary industry was 16,739.5 billion yuan, up by 11.3 percent; and that in the tertiary industry was 36,287.7 billion yuan, up by 2.1 percent. The private investment in fixed assets[40] was 30,765.9 billion yuan, up by 7.0 percent. The investment in infrastructure[41] increased by 0.4 percent. The investment in social sector[42] increased by 10.7 percent.

38. The figure of the investment in fixed assets in 2020 was revised according to the statistical survey method reform and programmes. The growth rates in 2021 were calculated on a comparable basis.

39. See Note 20.

40. Private investment in fixed assets refers to investment in the construction or purchase of fixed assets by domestic collective, private and individual-owned enterprises and organizations or their holding enterprises (including absolute holding and relative holding enterprises).

41. Investment in infrastructure includes investment in transportation, postal service, telecommunication, radio, TV and satellite transmission, internet and related services, water conservancy, environment and public facilities management.

42. Investment in social sector includes investment in education, heath and social services, culture, sports and recreation.

Figure 15: Shares of Investment in Fixed Assets of the Three Industries (Excluding Rural Households) in 2021

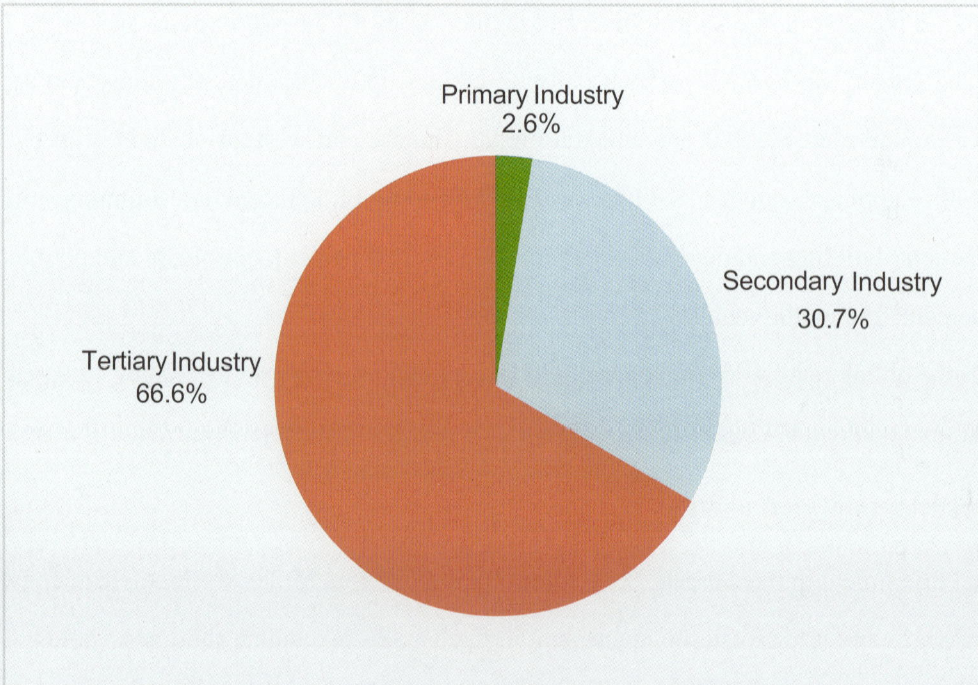

Table 6: Growth Rates of Investment in Fixed Assets (Excluding Rural Households) by Sectors in 2021

Sector	Increase over 2020 (%)	Sector	Increase over 2020 (%)
Total	**4.9**	Financial Intermediation	1.9
Agriculture,Forestry, Animal Husbandry and Fishery	9.3	Real Estate[43]	5.0
Mining	10.9	Leasing and Business Services	13.6
Manufacturing	13.5	Scientific Research and Technical Services	14.5
Production and Supply of Electricity, Heat Power, Gas and Water	1.1	Water Conservancy, Environment and Public Facilities Management	-1.2
Construction	1.6	Services to Households, Repair and Other Services	-10.3
Wholesale and Retail Trades	-5.9	Education	11.7
Transport, Storage and Post	1.6	Health and Social Services	19.5
Hotels and Catering Services	6.6	Culture, Sports and Entertainment	1.6
Information Transmission, Software and Information Technology Services	-12.1	Public Management, Social Security and Social Organizations	-38.2

43. The investment in real estate includes the investment in real estate development, construction of buildings for own use, property management, intermediary services and other real estate investment.

Table 7: Newly Increased Production and Operation Capacity through Fixed Assets Investment in 2021

Item	Unit	Volume
Newly increased power transformer equipment with a capacity of over 220 kilovolts	10,000 kilovolt-amperes	24334
New railways put into operation	kilometer	4208
Of which: high-speed railways	kilometer	2168
Extended or new double-track railways put into operation	kilometer	2769
Electrified railways put into operation	kilometer	4189
Length of new and rebuilt highways	kilometer	9028
New throughput capacity of berths for over 10,000-tonnage ships	10,000 tons/year	25368
New civil transportation airports	-	7
New lines of optical-fiber cables	10,000 km	319

In 2021, the investment in real estate development was 14,760.2 billion yuan, up by 4.4 percent over the previous year. Of this total, the investment in residential buildings reached 11,117.3 billion yuan, an increase of 6.4 percent, that in office buildings was 597.4 billion yuan, down by 8.0 percent, and that in buildings for commercial business was 1,244.5 billion yuan, down by 4.8 percent. The floor space of the commercial buildings for sale was 510.23 million square meters at the end of 2021, an increase of 11.73 million square meters over that at the end of 2020. The floor space of the commercial residential buildings for sale was 227.61 million square meters, an increase of 3.81 million square meters.

In 2021, 1.65 million housing units were started to be rebuilt in rundown urban areas nationwide and 2.05 million were basically completed. There were 0.94 million units of government-subsidized rental housing that were started to be built or made available.

Table 8: Main Indicators for Real Estate Development and Sales and Growth Rates in 2021

Item	Unit	Volume	Increase over 2020 (%)
Value of Investment	100 million RMB	147602	4.4
Of which: residential buildings	100 million RMB	111173	6.4
Floor space of buildings under construction	10000 square meters	975387	5.2
Of which: residential buildings	10000 square meters	690319	5.3
Floor space of buildings newly started	10000 square meters	198895	-11.4
Of which: residential buildings	10000 square meters	146379	-10.9
Floor space of buildings completed	10000 square meters	101412	11.2
Of which: residential buildings	10000 square meters	73016	10.8
Floor space of commercial buildings sold	10000 square meters	179433	1.9
Of which: residential buildings	10000 square meters	156532	1.1
Funds for investment this year	100 million RMB	201132	4.2
Of which: domestic loans	100 million RMB	23296	-12.7
individual mortgage	100 million RMB	32388	8.0

VII. Foreign Economic Relations

The total value of imports and exports of goods in 2021 reached 39,100.9 billion yuan, up by 21.4 percent over that of the previous year. Of this total, the value of goods exported was 21,734.8 billion yuan, up by 21.2 percent; the value of goods imported was 17,366.1 billion yuan, up by 21.5 percent. The surplus of trade in goods reached 4,368.7 billion yuan, up by 734.4 billion yuan over that of the previous year. The total value of imports and exports between China and countries along the Belt and Road[44] was 11,597.9 billion yuan, an increase of 23.6 percent over that of the previous year. Of the total, the value of goods exported was 6,592.4 billion yuan, an increase of 21.5 percent; that of goods imported was 5,005.5 billion yuan, an increase of 26.4 percent.

44. The Belt and Road refers to the Silk Road Economic Belt and the 21st Century Maritime Silk Road.

Figure 16: Total Value of Imports and Exports of Goods 2017-2021

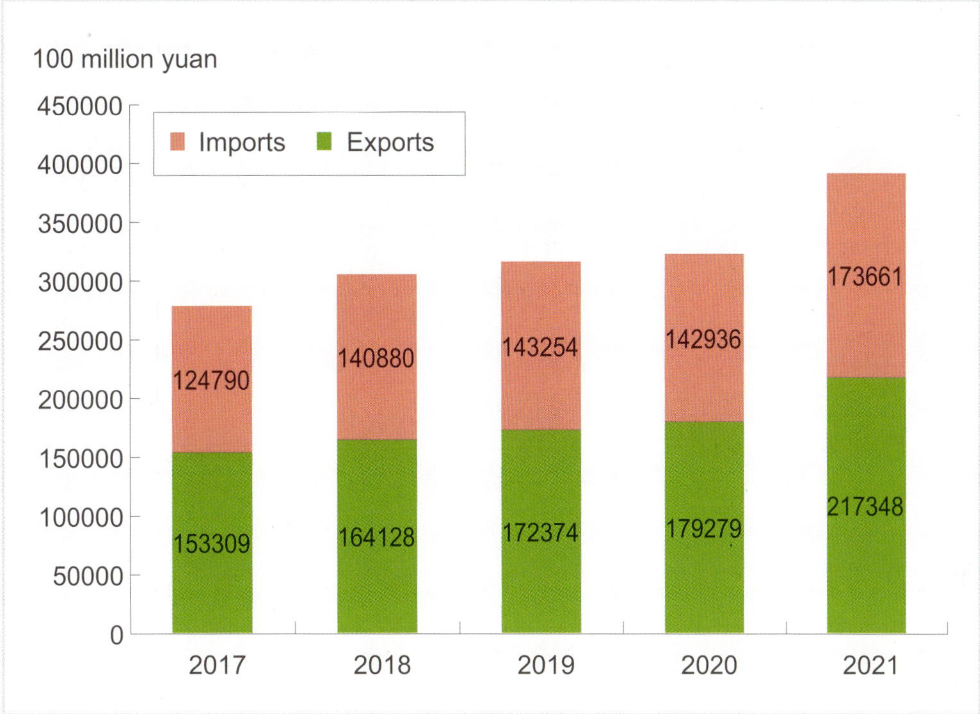

Table 9: Total Value and Growth Rates of Imports and Exports of Goods in 2021

Item	Value (100 million yuan)	Increase over 2020(%)
Total value of imports and exports of goods	**391009**	**21.4**
Exports	217348	21.2
Of which: General trade	132445	24.4
Processing trade	53378	9.9
Of which: Mechanical and electronic products	128286	20.4
High & new technology products	63266	17.9
Imports	173661	21.5
Of which: General trade	108395	25.0
Processing trade	31601	13.3
Of which: Mechanical and electronic products	73657	12.2
High & new technology products	54088	14.7
Trade surplus	**43687**	**20.2**

Table 10: Main Export Commodities in Volume and Value and the Growth Rates in 2021

Item	Unit	Volume	Increase over 2020 (%)	Value (100 million yuan)	Increase over 2020 (%)
Rolled steel	10000 tons	6690	24.6	5289	67.9
Textile yarns and textile articles	—	—	—	9384	-12.2
Clothes and clothing accessories	—	—	—	11000	15.6
Footwear	10000 pairs	873231	18.1	3097	26.2
Furniture and parts	—	—	—	4772	18.2
Luggage and similar containers	10000 tons	244	21.4	1800	26.1
Toys	—	—	—	2980	28.6
Plastic articles	—	—	—	6397	20.5
Integrated circuits	100 million pieces	3107	19.6	9930	23.4
Automatic data processing machines and components	—	—	—	16488	12.9
Mobile phones	10000 sets	95420	-1.2	9447	9.3
Containers	10000 units	484	144.0	1514	198.3
Liquid crystal display panels	10000 units	142439	12.4	1788	30.5
Motor vehicles (including chassis)	10000 sets	212	95.9	2227	104.6

Table 11: Main Import Commodities in Volume and Value and the Growth Rates in 2021

Item	Unit	Volume	Increase over 2020 (%)	Value (100 million yuan)	Increase over 2020 (%)
Soybean	10000 tons	9652	-3.8	3459	26.1
Edible vegetable oil	10000 tons	1039	-3.7	706	24.0
Iron ore and concentrate	10000 tons	112432	-3.9	11942	39.6
Coal and lignite	10000 tons	32322	6.6	2319	64.1
Crude oil	10000 tons	51298	-5.4	16618	34.4
Petroleum products refined	10000 tons	2712	-4.0	1078	31.6
Natural gas	10000 tons	12136	19.9	3601	56.3
Plastics in primary forms	10000 tons	3397	-16.4	3950	8.8
Paper pulp	10000 tons	2969	-2.7	1296	19.5
Rolled steel	10000 tons	1427	-29.5	1210	3.9
Unwrought copper and its alloys	10000 tons	553	-17.2	3387	12.5
Integrated circuits	100 million pieces	6355	16.9	27935	15.4
Motor vehicles (including chassis)	10000 sets	94	0.6	3489	7.6

Table 12: Imports and Exports of Goods by Major Countries and Regions, the Growth Rates and Proportions in 2021

Country or region	Exports (100 million yuan)	Increase over 2020 (%)	Proportion of the total (%)	Imports (100 million yuan)	Increase over 2020 (%)	Proportion of the total (%)
ASEAN	31255	17.7	14.4	25489	22.2	14.7
European Union	33483	23.7	15.4	20028	12.1	11.5
United States	37224	19.0	17.1	11603	24.2	6.7
Japan	10722	8.5	4.9	13298	10.1	7.7
Republic of Korea	9617	23.5	4.4	13791	15.1	7.9
Hong Kong, China	22641	20.3	10.4	627	30.2	0.4
Taiwan, China	5063	21.7	2.3	16146	16.5	9.3
Brazil	3464	43.4	1.6	7138	20.3	4.1
Russia	4364	24.7	2.0	5122	28.2	2.9
India	6302	36.6	2.9	1819	25.1	1.0
South Africa	1365	29.4	0.6	2147	49.4	1.2

The total value of imports and exports of services in 2021 was 5,298.3 billion yuan, up by 16.1 percent over that of the previous year. The export value of services was 2,543.5 billion yuan, up by 31.4 percent. The import value of services was 2,754.8 billion yuan, up by 4.8 percent. The trade deficit in imports and exports of services was 211.3 billion yuan.

The year 2021 witnessed the establishment of 47,643 enterprises with foreign direct investment (excluding banking, securities and insurance), up by 23.5 percent over that of the previous year, and the foreign direct investment actually utilized totaled 1,149.4 billion yuan, up by 14.9 percent, or 173.5 billion US dollars, up by 20.2 percent. Specifically, there were 5,336 newly established enterprises receiving direct investment from countries along the Belt and Road (including the investment in China via some free ports), up by 24.3 percent; and foreign capital directly invested in China reached 74.3 billion yuan, up by 29.4 percent, or 11.2 billion US dollars, up by 36.0 percent. In 2021, the foreign investment actually utilized by high technology industry reached 346.9 billion yuan, up by 17.1 percent, or 52.2 billion US dollars, up by 22.1 percent.

Table 13: Total Value of Foreign Direct Investment (Excluding Banking, Securities and Insurance) and the Growth Rates in 2021

Sector	Enterprises	Increase over 2020 (%)	Actually Utilized Value (100 million yuan)	Increase over 2020 (%)
Total	**47643**	**23.5**	**11494**	**14.9**
Of which: Agriculture, Forestry, Animal Husbandry and Fishery	491	-0.4	55	38.4
Manufacturing	4455	19.4	2216	2.8
Production and Supply of Electricity, Heat Power, Gas and Water	465	78.9	249	14.9
Transport, Storage and Post	693	17.1	351	1.3
Information Transmission, Software and Information Technology Services	4053	15.1	1345	18.8
Wholesale and Retail	13379	23.7	1098	34.1
Real Estate	1125	-5.5	1571	11.7
Leasing and Business Services	9290	23.7	2193	19.3
Services to Households, Repair and Other Services	522	16.8	31	44.6

In 2021, the non-financial outbound direct investment reached 733.2 billion yuan, down by 3.5 percent over that of the previous year, or 113.6 billion US dollars, up by 3.2 percent. Of this total, that to countries along the Belt and Road reached 20.3 billion US dollars, up by 14.1 percent.

Table 14: Total Value and Growth Rates of Non-financial Outbound Direct Investment in 2021

Sector	Value (100 million US dollars)	Increase over 2020 (%)
Total	**1136.4**	**3.2**
Of which: Agriculture, Forestry, Animal Husbandry and Fishery	11.3	-18.7
Mining	49.8	-2.2
Manufacturing	184.0	-7.9
Production and Supply of Electricity, Heat Power, Gas and Water	48.9	75.9
Construction	55.7	7.9
Wholesale and Retail	176.5	9.8
Transport, Storage and Post	51.0	92.5
Information Transmission, Software and Information Technology Services	75.3	12.2
Real Estate	24.9	-8.8
Leasing and Business Services	366.2	-12.4

In 2021, the accomplished business revenue through contracted overseas engineering projects was 999.6 billion yuan, down by 7.1 percent over that of the previous year, or 154.9 billion US dollars, down by 0.6 percent. Specifically, the accomplished business revenue from countries along the Belt and Road was 89.7 billion US dollars, a decrease of 1.6 percent, accounting for 57.9 percent of the accomplished business revenue through contracted overseas engineering projects. The number of labor forces sent abroad through overseas labor contracts was 320 thousand.

VIII. Finance and Financial Intermediation

The national general public budget revenue reached 20,253.9 billion yuan in 2021, up by 10.7 percent over that of the previous year, of which tax revenue amounted to 17,273.1 billion yuan, up by 11.9 percent. The national general public budget expenditure reached 24,632.2 billion yuan, up by 0.3 percent over that of the previous year. The newly added tax and fee cuts in 2021 was around 1.1 trillion yuan.

Figure 17: National General Public Budget Revenue 2017-2021

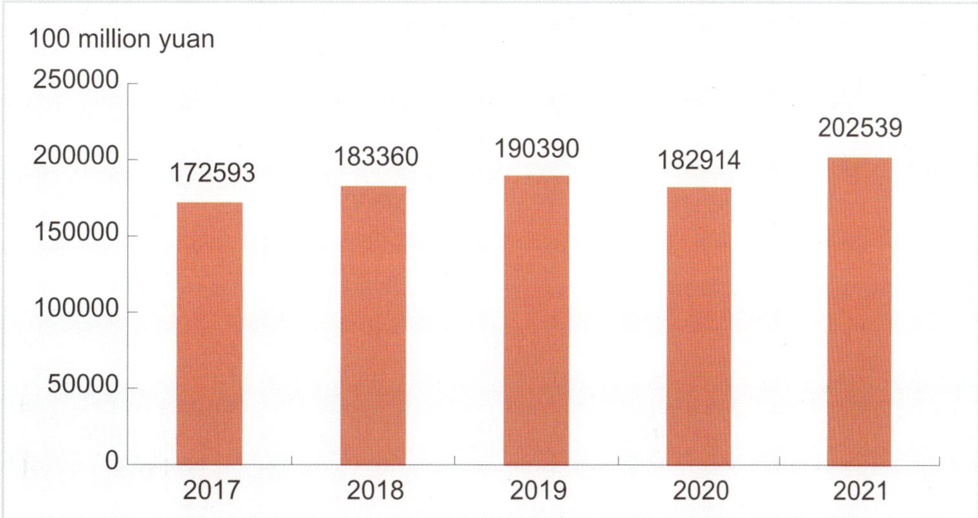

Note: Data for general public budget revenue from 2017 to 2020 as shown in the figure were final accounts and that of 2021 was the executive accounts.

By the end of 2021, money supply of broad sense (M_2) was 238.3 trillion yuan, an increase of 9.0 percent over that by the end of the previous year. Money supply of narrow sense (M_1) was 64.7 trillion yuan, up by 3.5 percent. Cash in circulation (M_0) was 9.1 trillion yuan, up by 7.7 percent.

In 2021, the aggregate financing to the real economy (AFRE) (flow)[45] reached 31.4 trillion yuan, or 3.4

45. The AFRE (flow) refers to the total volume of financing provided by the financial system to the real economy within a certain period of time.

trillion yuan less than that in 2020 on a comparable basis. The AFRE (stock)[46] totaled 314.1 trillion yuan at the end of 2021, up by 10.3 percent over that at the end of 2020 on a comparable basis. Specifically, loans granted to the real economy in Renminbi stood at 191.5 trillion yuan, up by 11.6 percent. Savings deposit in Renminbi and foreign currencies in all items of financial institutions totaled 238.6 trillion yuan at the end of 2021, an increase of 20.2 trillion yuan compared with that at the beginning of the year. Of this total, the savings deposit in Renminbi stood at 232.3 trillion yuan, an increase of 19.7 trillion yuan. Loans in Renminbi and foreign currencies in all items of financial institutions reached 198.5 trillion yuan, an increase of 20.1 trillion yuan. Of this total, loans in Renminbi were 192.7 trillion yuan, an increase of 19.9 trillion yuan. Inclusive finance loans in Renminbi[47] reached 26.5 trillion yuan, an increase of 5.0 trillion yuan.

Table 15: Savings Deposit and Loans in RMB and Foreign Currencies in All Financial Institutions and Growth Rates at the End of 2021

Item	Year-end figure (100 million yuan)	Increase over 2020 (%)
Savings deposit	**2386062**	**9.3**
Domestic households	1033118	10.6
Deposits in RMB	1025012	10.7
Domestic non-financial enterprises	730137	6.1
Loans	**1985108**	**11.3**
Domestic short-term loans	520506	5.7
Domestic medium- and long-term loans	1291149	13.5

Loans in Renminbi from rural financial institutions (rural credit cooperatives, rural cooperation banks and rural commercial banks) totaled 24,249.6 billion yuan by the end of 2021, an increase of 2,660.7 billion yuan as compared with that at the beginning of the year. Loans in Renminbi for consumption use from all financial institutions totaled 54,884.9 billion yuan, an increase of 5,318.1 billion yuan. Of the total, short-term personal loans totaled 9,355.8 billion yuan, an increase of 608.0 billion yuan, and medium- and long-term personal loans reached 45,529.2 billion yuan, an increase of 4,710.1 billion yuan.

46. The AFRE (stock) refers to the outstanding financing provided by the financial system to the real economy at the end of a period of time (a month, a quarter or a year).

47. Inclusive finance loans include loans to micro and small businesses with single-client credit line under 10 million yuan, operating loans to self-employed businesses and owners of micro and small businesses, producing and operating loans to farmers, consumption loans to registered people living in poverty, venture guarantee loans and student loans.

Funds raised through A-shares issued on Shanghai and Shenzhen Stock Exchanges[48] amounted to 1,674.3 billion yuan in 2021, an increase of 132.6 billion yuan from the previous year. 481 A-shares were newly issued on Shanghai and Shenzhen Stock Exchanges, raising 535.1 billion yuan worth of capital altogether, up by 60.9 billion yuan over that of the previous year. Of the total, 162 shares were from the science and technology innovation board, raising 202.9 billion yuan; refinancing of A-shares on Shanghai and Shenzhen Stock Exchanges (including public newly issued, targeted placement, right issued, preferred stock and exchanged convertible bonds) raised 1,139.1 billion yuan, an increase of 71.7 billion yuan over that of the previous year. 11 shares were publicly issued on Beijing Stock Exchanges, raising[49] 2.1 billion yuan. Various types of market entities financed 8,655.3 billion yuan through issuing bonds (including corporate bonds, convertible bonds, exchangeable bonds, financial bonds issued by policy banks, local government bonds and asset-backed securities) on Shanghai and Shenzhen Stock Exchanges, up by 177.6 billion yuan over that of the previous year. There were 6,932 companies listed on National Equities Exchange and Quotations[50] and funds raised by listed companies reached 26.0 billion yuan in 2021.

In 2021, the issuance of corporate credit bonds[51] reached 14.7 trillion yuan, an increase of 0.5 trillion yuan over that of the previous year.

The premium of primary insurance received by the insurance companies[52] totaled 4,490.0 billion yuan in 2021, up by 4.0 percent over that of the previous year on a comparable basis. Of this total, life insurance premium of primary insurance amounted to 2,357.2 billion yuan, health and casualty insurance premium of primary insurance 965.7 billion yuan, and property insurance premium of primary insurance 1,167.1 billion yuan. Insurance companies paid an indemnity worth of 1,560.9 billion yuan, of which life insurance indemnity was 354.0 billion yuan, health and casualty insurance indemnity 438.1 billion yuan, and property insurance indemnity 768.7 billion yuan.

---

48. Funds raised through Shanghai and Shenzhen Stock Exchanges are calculated by the money raised on the listing date, and the funds raised include the actual exchanged convertible bonds, which were 119.5 billion yuan in 2020 and 134.2 billion yuan in 2021.

49. Funds raised through Beijing Stock Exchanges are calculated by the money raised on the listing date. The funds raised only include those by newly-listed companies since the opening of the Beijing Stock Exchanges. Historical data of funds raised by Select Tier companies transferred to the Beijing Stock Exchange remained in the statistical form of the National Equities Exchange and Quotations.

50.National Equities Exchange and Quotations, also called "the New Over-the-Counter Market", is a national securities exchange established upon approval by the State Council in 2012. Preferred stocks were excluded from funds raised by listed companies in National Equities Exchange and Quotations. Funds raised by shares are calculated by the disclosure date of the issurance report.

51.Corporate credit bonds include debt financing instruments issued by non-financial businesses, enterprise bonds, corporate bonds and convertible bonds.

52.The premium of primary insurance received by the insurance companies refers to the premium income from primary insurance contracts confirmed by the insurance companies.

IX. Households Income and Consumption and Social Security

In 2021, the per capita disposable income nationwide was 35,128 yuan, an increase of 9.1 percent over that of the previous year or a real increase of 8.1 percent after deducting price factors. The median[53] of per capita disposable income nationwide was 29,975 yuan, up by 8.8 percent. In terms of usual residence, the per capita disposable income of urban households was 47,412 yuan, up by 8.2 percent over that of 2020, or a real growth of 7.1 percent after deducting price factors. The median of per capita disposable income of urban households was 43,504 yuan, up by 7.7 percent. The per capita disposable income of rural households was 18,931 yuan, up by 10.5 percent over that of the previous year, or 9.7 percent in real terms after deducting price factors. The median of per capita disposable income of rural households was 16,902 yuan, up by 11.2 percent. The urban-rural per capita disposable income ratio was 2.50, narrowed by 0.06 over that of the previous year. Grouped by income quintile[54], the per capita disposable income of low-income group reached 8,333 yuan, the lower-middle-income group 18,445 yuan, the middle-income group 29,053 yuan, the upper-middle-income group 44,949 yuan and the high-income group 85,836 yuan. The per capita monthly income of migrant workers was 4,432 yuan, increased by 8.8 percent over that of the previous year. In 2021, the per capita disposable income of rural households from counties lifted out of poverty[55] was 14,051 yuan, up by 11.6 percent over that of 2020, or a real growth of 10.8 percent after deducting price factors.

The national per capita consumption expenditure was 24,100 yuan, up by 13.6 percent over that of the previous year, or a real increase of 12.6 percent after deducting price factors. Specifically, the per capita consumption expenditure on services[56] totaled 10,645 yuan, up by 17.8 percent over that of the previous year, accounting for 44.2 percent of the per capita consumption expenditure. In terms of usual residence, the per capita consumption expenditure of urban households was 30,307 yuan, up by 12.2 percent, or 11.1 percent in real terms after deducting price factors. The per capita consumption expenditure of rural households was 15,916 yuan, up by 16.1 percent, or a real increase of 15.3 percent after deducting price factors. The national Engel's Coefficient stood at 29.8 percent, with that of urban and rural households standing at 28.6 percent and 32.7 percent respectively.

---

53. The premium of primary insurance received by the insurance companies refers to the premium income from primary insurance contracts confirmed by the insurance companies.

54. The income quintile refers to the five equal partitions of all surveyed households, who are ranked from low to high based on per capita income level. The top 20 percent with the highest income are classified as high-income group, and the other four levels are upper-middle-income group, middle-income group, lower-middle-income group and low-income group.

55. Counties lifted out of poverty include 832 key counties under the national poverty alleviation and development program and counties in contiguous poor areas as well as 7 cities and counties in Aksu prefecture, Xinjiang.

56. The consumption expenditure on services refers to the spending by households on services for daily lives including catering, education, culture and recreation and medical services.

Figure 18: National Per Capita Disposable Income and Its Growth Rates 2017-2021

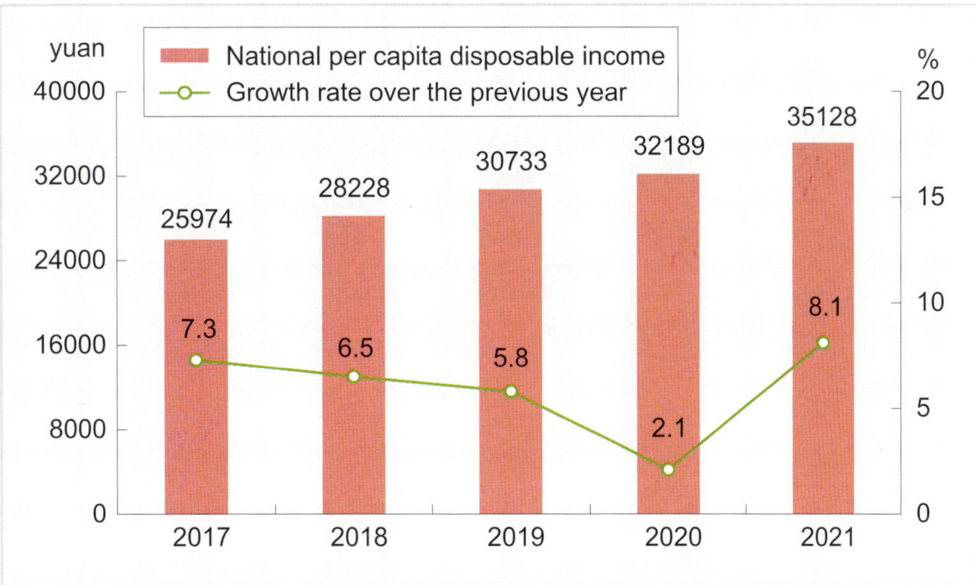

Figure 19: National Per Capita Consumption Expenditure and Composition in 2021

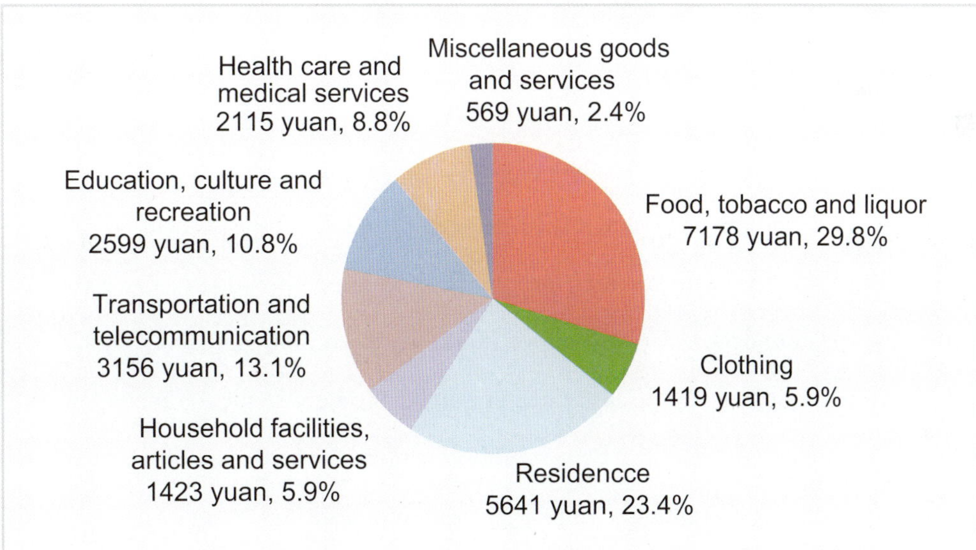

By the end of 2021, a total of 480.75 million people participated in basic endowment insurance program for urban workers, an increase of 24.54 million over that by the end of 2020. A total of 547.97 million people participated in basic endowment insurance program for urban and rural residents, an increase of 5.54 million. A total of 1,364.24 million people participated in basic medical insurance program, an increase of 2.93 million. Of this total, 354.22 million people participated in the program for workers, an increase of

9.67 million, and 1,010.02 million people participated in the program for urban and rural residents. A total of 229.58 million people participated in unemployment insurance program, an increase of 12.68 million. The number of people receiving unemployment insurance payment stood at 2.59 million by the end of 2021. A total of 282.84 million people participated in work-related injury insurance, an increase of 15.21 million, of which 90.86 million were migrant workers, an increase of 1.52 million. A total of 238.51 million people participated in maternity insurance programs, an increase of 2.83 million. By the end of 2021, minimum living allowances were granted to 7.38 million urban residents and 34.74 million rural residents, and 4.38 million rural residents living in extreme poverty[57] received relief and assistance and 10.89 million people received temporary assistance[58]. National subsidies and allowances were provided to 8.17 million veterans and other entitled people in 2021.

By the end of 2021, there were altogether 43 thousand social welfare institutions providing accommodation, of which 40 thousand were elderly care institutions and 801 were institutions for child welfare, assistance and protection. The social welfare institutions provided 8.402 million beds[59], of which 8.135 million were for the elderly and 96 thousand were for children. By the end of 2021, there were 29 thousand community service centers and 472 thousand community service stations.

X. Science & Technology and Education

Expenditures on research and experimental development activities (R&D) were worth 2,786.4 billion yuan in 2021, up by 14.2 percent over that of 2020, accounting for 2.44 percent of GDP. Of this total, 169.6 billion yuan was used for basic research programs. A total of 48,700 projects were financed by the National Natural Science Foundation. By the end of 2021, there were altogether 533 state key laboratories in operation, 191 national engineering research centers under the new sequence management, 1,636 state-level enterprise technology centers and 212 demonstration centers for business startups and innovation. The National Fund for Technology Transfer and Commercialization established 36 sub-funds, with the total funds

57. Rural residents living in extreme poverty refer to the aged, the disabled and the minor under 16 years of age in rural areas who have no ability to work, no sources of income and no statutory obligors to provide for them, bring them up or support them, or whose statutory obligors have no ability to fulfill their obligations.

58. Temporary assistance refers to emergent and transitional assistance the government provides to families or individuals who experience hardships because of emergencies, unexpected harm, major diseases or other unusual factors and are not covered by other forms of social assistance programs or still suffer hardships after receiving other social assistance programs.

59. The beds provided by social welfare institutions include beds provided by adoption agencies, aid agencies and community agencies.

reaching 62.4 billion yuan. There were 1,287 state-level technology business incubators[60], and 2,551 national mass makerspaces[61]. A total of 4,601 thousand patents were authorized, up by 26.4 percent over that of the previous year. The number of PCT patent applications accepted[62] was 73 thousand. By the end of 2021, the number of valid patents was 15,421 thousand, of which 2,704 thousand were domestic valid invention patents. The number of high-value invention patents per 10,000 people[63] was 7.5. Trademark registration totaled 7,739 thousand, up by 34.3 percent over that of the previous year. A total of 670 thousand technology transfer contracts were signed, representing 3,729.4 billion yuan in value, up by 32.0 percent over that of the previous year.

Figure 20: The Expenditure on Research and Experimental Development Activities (R&D) and Its Growth Rates 2017-2021

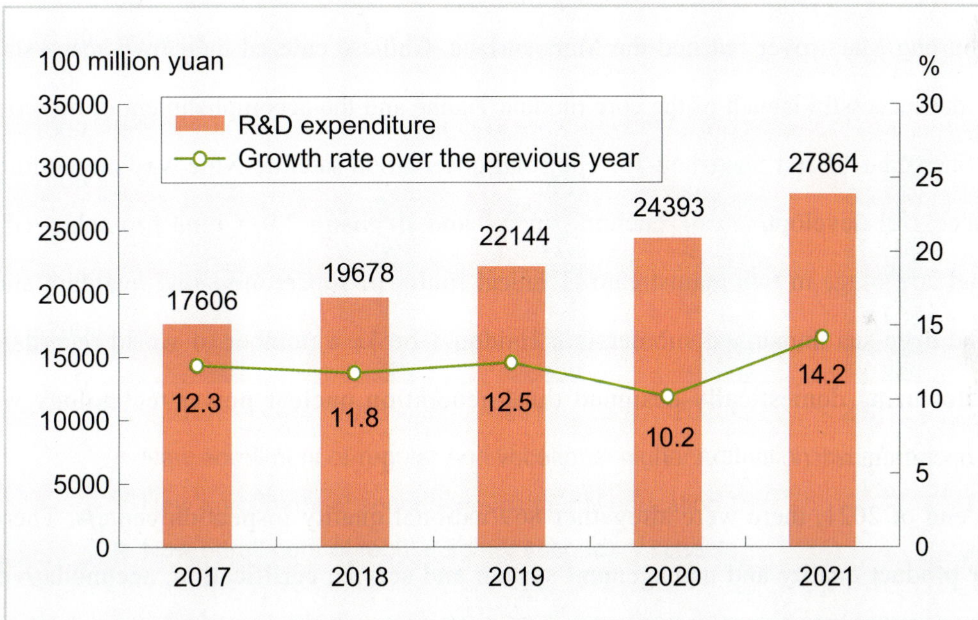

60. The state-level technology business incubators are technology-based business startup service providers consistent with the Administrative Measures for Technology Business Incubators that provide physical space, shared facilities and professional services with the mission of advancing transformation of technological achievements, cultivating technological enterprises and fostering the entrepreneurial spirit. They should be approved and accredited by the Ministry of Science and Technology.

61. The national mass makerspaces are new service platform for entrepreneurship and innovation that are in conformity with the Guidelines on Developing Mass Makerspaces and are reviewed and registered by the Ministry of Science and Technology in accordance with the Provisional Registration Regulations on National Mass Makerspaces.

62. The number of PCT patent applications accepted refers to the number of PCT patent application accepted by the State Intellectual Property Office which acts as the receiving office of PCT patent application. PCT is the abbreviation of Patent Cooperation Treaty, which is a treaty for international cooperation in the field of patents.

63.The number of high-value invention patents per 10,000 people refers to the number of valid invention patents owned per 10,000 national residents which are authorized by the China National Intellectual Property Administration and satisfy any of the following conditions: invention patents for strategic emerging industries; invention patents having corresponding foreign patents; invention patents maintained more than 10 years; invention patents with a relatively high pledge financing amount; and invention patents that won the National Science and Technology Award and the China Patent Award.

episodes of 194 TV series and 78,372 minutes of TV cartoons were made in 2021. The country produced 565 feature movies and 175 popular science movies, documentaries, animation and special movies[68]. A total of 27.6 billion copies of newspapers and 2.0 billion copies of magazines were issued, and 11.0 billion copies of books were published. The average number of books possessed per person[69] was 7.76 copies. By the end of the year, there were 4,233 archives in China and 189.31 million files were made accessible to the public. The business revenue of enterprises above the designated size engaged in culture and related industries reached 11,906.4 billion yuan, up by 16.0 percent over that of the previous year on a comparable basis.

The year 2021 registered 3.25 billion domestic tourists, up by 12.8 percent over that of the previous year. Of this total, there were 2.34 billion tourists from urban areas, an increase of 13.4 percent; and 900 million tourists from rural areas, an increase of 11.1 percent. Domestic tourism revenue was 2,919.1 billion yuan, up by 31.0 percent. Of this total, tourists from urban areas spent 2,364.4 billion yuan, up by 31.6 percent; and tourists from rural areas spent 554.7 billion yuan, up by 28.4 percent.

Figure 22: The Person-times of Domestic Tourists and Its Growth Rates 2017-2021

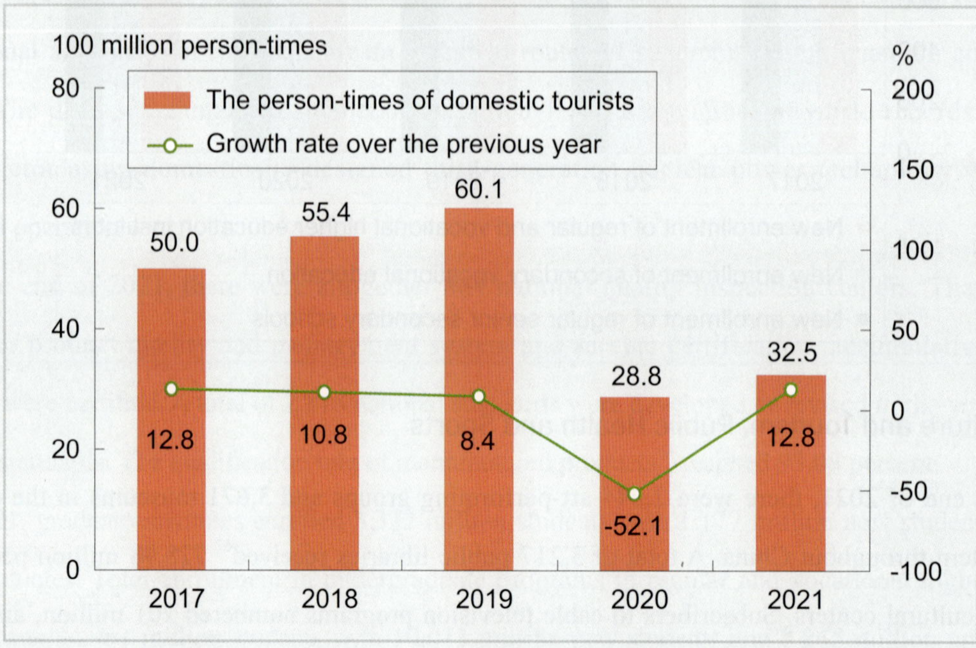

68. Special movies refer to those using different display modes in terms of projection techniques, equipment and program as compared with the ordinary cinemas, such as IMAX movies, 3D movies, 4D movies, multidimensional movies and full dome movies.

69. The average number of books possessed per person refers to the average number of books published in the year that can be possessed per person in China.

By the end of 2021, there were 1,031,000 medical and health institutions in China, including 37,000 hospitals. Of all the hospitals, 12,000 were public, and 25,000 were private. Of the 977,000 medical and health institutions at grass-root level, there were 35,000 town and township health centers, 36,000 community health service centers, 307,000 clinics and 599,000 village clinics. Of the 13,000 professional public health institutions, 3,380 were disease control and prevention centers and 2,790 were health monitoring institutions. By the end of 2021, there were 11.23 million medical technical personnel in China, including 4.27 million licensed doctors and licensed assistant doctors and 5.02 million registered nurses. The medical and health institutions in China possessed 9.57 million beds, of which hospitals possessed 7.48 million and township health centers had 1.44 million. The total number of medical visits[70] and hospital discharges[71] in 2021 reached 8.53 billion and 240 million respectively. By the end of 2021, a total of 102,314 confirmed cases of COVID-19 had been reported nationwide, 94,792 infected had been cured and discharged from hospital, and 4,636 people died. A total of 2,835.33 million doses of COVID-19 vaccines have been administered nationwide. A total of 11,937 medical and health institutions across the country provided nucleic acid testing services, with daily nucleic acid testing capacity reached 41.68 million.

Figure 23: Year-end Number of Medical Technical Personnel 2017-2021

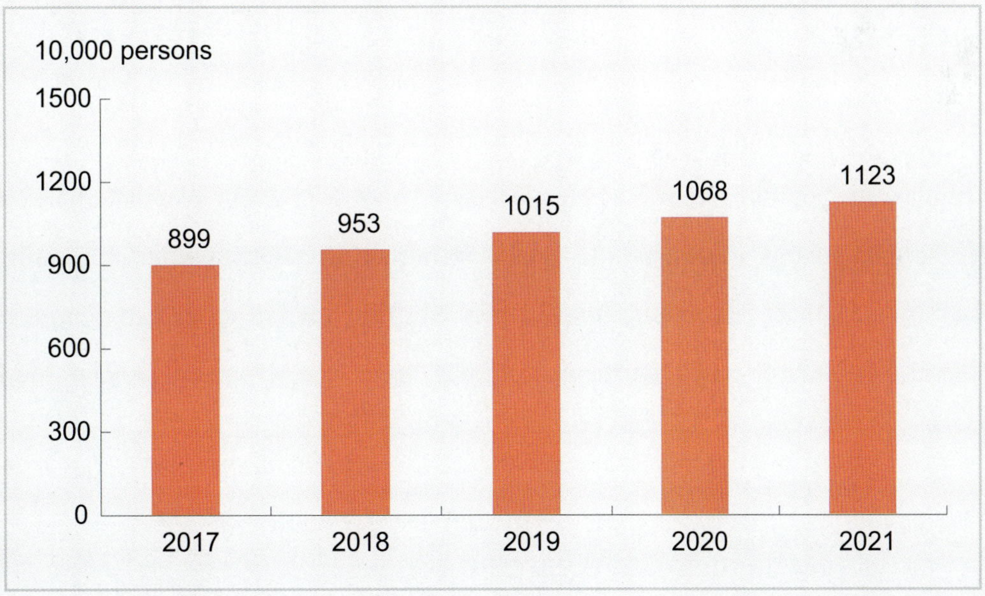

70. The total number of medical visits refers to the number of people receiving medical services, including outpatient services, emergency treatment, home visits, appointment-based diagnosis and treatment, health check-up of a specific item, and health consultation and guidance (excluding health lectures and nucleic acid tests).

71. The number of hospital discharges refers to the number of inpatients discharged from hospitals in the reporting period, including those who are discharged from hospitals or transferred to other medical institutions following doctors' advice, discharged from hospitals without doctors' permission, dead or other situations. The number of people who are recovered from family sickbeds is excluded.

There were altogether 3.971 million sports venues[72]. The sports venue area[73] totaled 3.41 billion square meters and the per capita sports venue area was 2.41 square meters. In 2021, Chinese athletes won 67 world championships in 16 sports events and broke 12 world records. At the 32nd Olympic Games, Chinese athletes won 38 gold medals and a total of 88 medals, ranking the second in the Olympic gold medal tally and overall medal count. Chinese physically-challenged athletes won 110 world championships in 5 international sports competitions. At the 16th Paralympic Games, Chinese athletes won 96 gold medals and a total of 207 medals, topped the gold medal tally and overall medal count for the fifth consecutive time.

XII. Resources, Environment and Emergency Management

In 2021, the total supply of state-owned land for construction use[74] was 690 thousand hectares, an increase of 4.8 percent over that of the previous year. Of this total, the land supply for industry, mining and warehousing was 175 thousand hectares, up by 4.9 percent; that for real estate[75] was 136 thousand hectares, down by 12.2 percent; and that for infrastructure facilities was 379 thousand hectares, up by 12.7 percent.

The total stock of water resources in 2021 was 2,952.0 billion cubic meters. With an increase of 1.9 percent over 2020, the total water consumption reached 592.1 billion cubic meters, of which water consumption for living purposes up by 5.3 percent, for industrial use up by 2.0 percent, for agricultural use up by 0.9 percent, and artificial recharge for environmental and ecological use grew by 2.9 percent. Water consumption per 10,000 yuan of GDP[76] was 54 cubic meters, a decline of 5.8 percent over that of the previous year. Water consumption per 10,000 yuan of industrial value added was 31 cubic meters, down by 7.0 percent. Per capita water consumption was 419 cubic meters, up by 1.8 percent over that of the previous year.

In 2021, the total area of afforestation reached 3.60 million hectares, of which 1.34 million hectares were afforested by manpower, accounting for 37.1 percent of the total. The land area improved by grass plantation[77] was 3.07 million hectares. By the end of 2021, there were 474 national natural reserves and 5

---

72. The sports venues belonging to armed forces and railway system are excluded in the census on sports venues.

73. The sports venue area refers to area used for physical training, sports competitions and physical fitness.

74. Total supply of state-owned land for construction use refers to the total amount of state-owned land for construction use with the land-use right transferred, allocated or leased to units or individuals through signed transaction contracts and allocation decisions by the municipal or county governments according to annual land supply plan and in line with relevant laws in the reporting period.

75. Land used for real estate refers to the sum of land used for commercial service and for residence.

76. The water consumption per 10,000 yuan of GDP and water consumption per 10,000 yuan of industrial value added are calculated at prices of 2020.

77. The land area improved by grass plantation refers to the area of increased forage grass by adopting measures such as sowing and cultivation plus the area where primitive vegetation and the ecology of grasslands have been improved by measures such as restraining the content of salt, alkali and sand, improving the quality of soil and fencing the forests.

national parks. A total of 62 thousand square kilometers of land have been saved from soil erosion.

Preliminary estimation indicated that the total energy consumption in 2021 amounted to 5.24 billion tons of standard coal equivalent, up by 5.2 percent over that of 2020. The consumption of coal increased by 4.6 percent; crude oil, up by 4.1 percent; natural gas, up by 12.5 percent; and electric power, up by 10.3 percent. The consumption of coal accounted for 56.0 percent of the total energy consumption, 0.9 percentage point lower than that of 2020, while clean energy consumption, such as natural gas, hydropower, nuclear power, wind power and solar power accounted for 25.5 percent, 1.2 percentage points higher. The comprehensive energy consumption per unit calcium carbide by key energy-intensive industrial enterprises went down by 5.3 percent, per unit synthetic ammonia was the same as that of last year, per ton steel down by 0.4 percent and per unit electrolytic aluminium down by 2.1 percent. The standard coal consumption per kilowatt-hour of thermal power generation decreased by 0.5 percent. The carbon dioxide emission per 10,000 yuan worth of GDP[78] was cut by 3.8 percent.

Figure 24: The Proportion of Clean Energy Consumption in the Total Energy Consumption 2017-2021

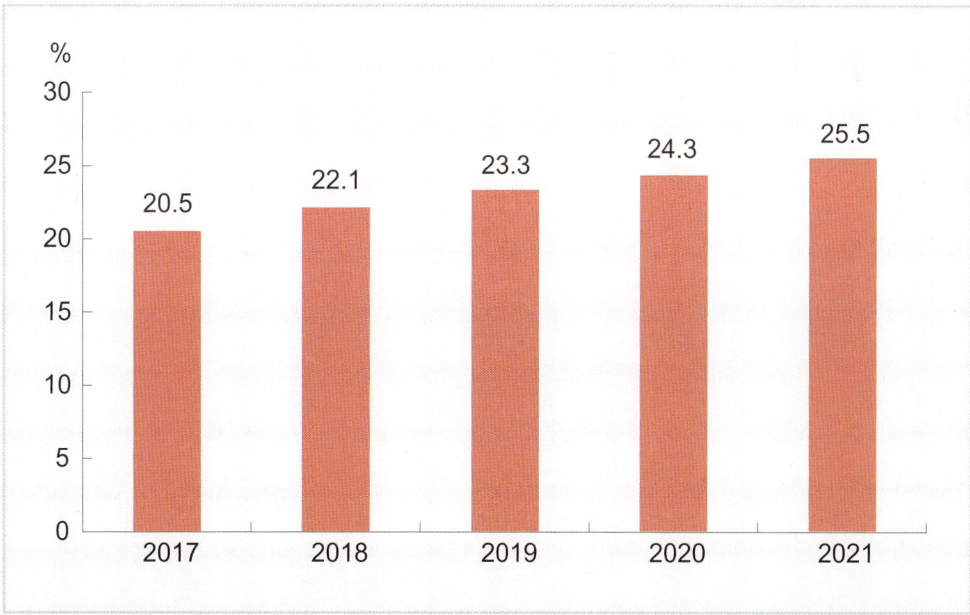

Area of offshore oceanic water[79] met the national quality standard Grade I and II accounted for 81.3 percent; that met Grade III standard 5.2 percent; and water of Grade IV or inferior quality 13.5 percent.

78. The carbon dioxide emission per 10,000 yuan worth of GDP is calculated at prices of 2020.
79. Offshore oceanic water quality is evaluated by the area method.

Of the 324 cities subject to urban regional daytime acoustic environment monitoring, 4.9 percent enjoyed excellent environment, 61.7 percent had good environment, 31.5 percent had average environment, and 1.9 percent had poor environment in 2021.

The average temperature in 2021 was 10.53℃, up by 0.28℃ compared with that of the previous year. Typhoons hit China 5 times in 2021.

In 2021, natural disasters hit 11.74 million hectares of crops, of which 1.63 million hectares of crops were demolished. Flood, waterlogging and geological disasters caused a direct economic loss of 247.7 billion yuan. Droughts caused a direct economic loss of 20.1 billion yuan. Disasters caused by low temperature, frost and snow made a total direct economic loss of 13.3 billion yuan. Oceanic disasters caused a direct economic loss of 3.0 billion yuan. The country recorded 20 earthquakes with magnitude 5.0 and over, causing a direct economic loss about 10.7 billion yuan. The year 2021 witnessed 616 forest fires, with 4 thousand hectares of forests damaged.

The death toll due to work accidents amounted to 26,307 people. Work accidents in industrial, mining and commercial companies caused 1.374 deaths out of every 100 thousand employees, up by 5.6 percent over that of 2020. The death toll for one million tons of coal produced in coalmines was 0.045 people, down by 23.7 percent. The road traffic death toll per 10 thousand vehicles was 1.57 people, down by 5.4 percent.

Data Sources:

In this Communiqué, data of newly increased employed people in urban areas, registered unemployment rate in urban areas, social security, unemployment insurance, work injury insurance and skilled workers schools are from the Ministry of Human Resources and Social Security; data of foreign exchange reserves and exchange rates are from the State Administration of Foreign Exchange; data of market entities, quality inspection, the formulation and revision of national standards and qualification rate of manufactured products are from the State Administration for Market Regulation; data of environment monitoring are from the Ministry of Ecology and Environment; data of output of aquatic products and area of farmland newly equipped with effective water-saving irrigation systems are from the Ministry of Agriculture and Rural Affairs; data of production of timber, area of afforestation, area of grass planting and improvement, national natural reserves and national parks are from the National Forestry and Grassland Administration; data of area of farmland newly equipped with irrigation system, water resources, water consumption and land newly saved from soil erosion are from the Ministry of Water Resources; data of installed power generation capacity, new power transformer equipment with a capacity of 220 kilovolts and above and electricity consumption are from the China Electricity Council; data of volume of freight handled by ports, container shipping of ports, highway transportation, waterway transportation, new and rebuilt highways and new throughput capacity of berths for over 10,000-tonnage ships are from the Ministry of Transport; data of railway transportation, new railways put into operation, new double-track railways put into operation and electrified railways put into operation are from China Railway; data of civil aviation and new civil transportation airports are from the Civil Aviation Administration of China; data of pipeline transportation are from China National Petroleum Cooperation, China Petrochemical Cooperation, China National Offshore Oil Cooperation and China Oil & Gas Piping Network Cooperation; data of motor vehicles for civilian use and traffic accidents are from the Ministry of Public Security; data of postal service are from the State Post Bureau; data of telecommunication, software revenue, and new lines of optical-fiber cables are from the Ministry of Industry and Information Technology; data of internet users and internet coverage are from China Internet Network Information Center; data of housing units rebuilt or renovated in rundown urban areas and government-subsidized rental housing are from the Ministry of Housing and Urban-Rural Development; data of imports and exports of goods are from the General Administration of Customs; data of imports and exports of services, foreign direct investment, outbound direct investment, overseas contracted projects and overseas labor contracts are from the Ministry of Commerce; data of finance are from the Ministry of Finance; data of newly added tax and fee cuts are from the State Taxation Administration; data of monetary finance and corporate credit bonds are from the People's Bank of China; data of funds raised through domestic exchange markets are from China Securities Regulatory Commission; data of the insurance sector are from China Banking and Insurance Regulatory Commission; data of medical insurance and maternity insurance are from the National Healthcare and Security Administration; data of urban and rural minimum living allowances, relief and assistance granted to rural residents living in extreme poverty, temporary assistance and social welfare are from the Ministry of Civil Affairs; data of entitled people are from the Ministry of Veterans Affairs; data of natural science foundation projects are from the National Natural Science Foundation; data of state key laboratories, National Fund for Technology Transfer and Commercialization, state-level technology business incubators, national mass makerspaces and technology transfer contracts are from the Ministry of Science and Technology; data of national engineering research centers, enterprise technical centers and demonstration centers for business startups and innovation are from the National Development and Reform Commission; data of patents and trademarks are from the National Intellectual Property Administration;

data of satellite launches are from the State Administration of Science, Technology and Industry for National Defense; data of education are from the Ministry of Education; data of art-performing groups, museums, public libraries, cultural centers and tourism are from the Ministry of Culture and Tourism; data of television and radio programs are from the National Radio and Television Administration; data of movies are from the China Film Administration; data of newspapers, magazines and books are from the National Press and Publication Administration; data of files are from the State Archives Administration; data of medical care and health are from the National Health Commission; data of sports are from the General Administration of Sport; data of physically-challenged athletes are from the China Disabled Persons' Federation; data of supply of state-owned land for construction use and direct economic loss caused by oceanic disasters are from the Ministry of Natural Resources; data of average temperature and typhoons are from the China Meteorological Administration; data of areas of crops hit by natural disasters, direct economic loss caused by flood, waterlogging and geological disasters, direct economic loss caused by droughts, direct economic loss caused by low temperature, frost and snow, the number of earthquakes, direct economic loss caused by earthquakes, forest fires, areas of forests damaged and workplace accidents are from the Ministry of Emergency Management; all the other data are from the National Bureau of Statistics.

In case of any differences between English translation and the original Chinese text, the Chinese edition shall prevail.